ENDINGS

—— AND ——

BEGINNINGS

Law, Medicine, and Society
in Assisted Life and Death

Larry I. Palmer

PRAEGER

Westport, Connecticut
London

KF 3827
E 87
P 35
2000

Library of Congress Cataloging-in-Publication Data

Palmer, Larry I., 1944–
   Endings and beginnings : law, medicine, and society in assisted life and death /
Larry I. Palmer.
    p. cm.
   Includes bibliographical references and index.
   ISBN 0–275–96681–X (alk. paper)
   1. Right to die—United States. 2. Assisted suicide—Law and legislation—United
States. 3. Human reproductive technology—Law and legislation—United States.
4. Euthanasia—United States. 5. Human reproductive technology. 6. Terminal
care. I. Title.
KF3827.E87 P35 2000
344.73'04197—dc21   99–054876

British Library Cataloguing in Publication Data is available.

Library of Congress Catalog Card Number: 99–054876
ISBN: 0–275–96681–X

First published in 2000

Praeger Publishers, 88 Post Road West, Westport, CT 06881
An imprint of Greenwood Publishing Group, Inc.
www.praeger.com

Printed in the United States of America

The paper used in this book complies with the
Permanent Paper Standard issued by the National
Information Standards Organization (Z39.48–1984).

10 9 8 7 6 5 4 3 2 1

For Suzy

Contents

Acknowledgments

To create a public space where legal analyses of abortion, reproductive technology, or cloning can be discussed with my students, I have discovered I must rely upon their intuitive respect for the uniqueness of each others' family experiences. I have attempted to create a context for public discourse in which no one need reveal his or her own experience with or fears about abortion, adoption, infertility, child abuse, sexual orientation or confusion, or inadequacy as a parent. The further challenge is how these intimate discussions are translated into public arguments, policies, or laws without denigrating those who hold conflicting or divergent views about these most personal matters.

The arguments about law and medicine I make in this book are influenced not only by my professional experience, but also, perhaps involuntarily, by my being a 55-year-old husband and father, as well as a son in an African American family with nine brothers and sisters. As the ninth child in this extended family, I have listened many times to my siblings' stories of my own birth at home. My father's sudden but expected death from a heart attack (after several years of hypertension and several minor strokes) came when I was a law student. Twenty years later, the six-month ordeal of my mother's death from cancer as I was completing my first book on law and medicine created a similar sense of emotional loss, but also a host of ethical dilemmas for me and my siblings. I have used the protracted debate over physician-assisted suicide to provide a new analysis of law and medicine that ushers in a new era in our civic discourse and provides a means of restoring a sense of community.

I wish to acknowledge the support of my colleagues at Cornell Law School for providing me with an environment in which to write, and stimulating students with whom I have engaged some of the ideas contained in this book. I also would like to recognize the generosity of the law school in its financial support as well as former Dean Russell K. Osgood and interim Dean Charles W. Wolfram, who provided summer research stipends. A special word of thanks to Jennifer L. Smith, who provided careful assistance in the production of this book's many drafts.

I wish to thank the staff at Cornell's various libraries for their cheerful assistance in locating materials. I also wish to thank Heather Staines, my acquisitions editor, and Rebecca Ardwin, my production editor, at Praeger Publishers, for the care with which they handled this project.

Institutions and colleagues elsewhere provided me with opportunities to discuss some of the ideas in earlier incarnations of this book: a lecture at Deep Springs College in 1994; the Holland Lecture at Washington State University in 1995; a talk to the Seminar on Science, Ethics, and Public Policy at the California Institute of Technology in 1996; and the Rome Lecture at the University of Maryland School of Law in 1996.

Four individuals were generous in providing me with comments on various drafts of the entire manuscript: Davydd J. Greenwood, as he has for nearly twenty years, provided me with invaluable insights. Roberta R. Armstrong's keen eye for concise language greatly improved the manuscript. Janet L. Dolgin provided encouragement and inspiration by providing comments and sharing her published and unpublished work with me regarding the family. My wife, Suzy Szasz, has given me not only the benefit of her thoughts and comments, but also the daily sense of intellectual companionship that allowed this project to be completed. This work is dedicated to her.

Introduction

Law ... should more properly serve as a means to preserve the diversity of the communities of meaning.

Stephen L. Carter[1]

Faith in medical progress has created public dilemmas at both the beginning and end of life. The collective search for meaning in our large and complex society fails to acknowledge the influence of basic social institutions—family, religion, science, medicine, and law—in shaping its intimate concepts. Too often individuals have turned to law, and particularly the United States Supreme Court, to provide some guidance in their search for community. Science also appears to offer guidance. Faith in scientific progress and its alliance with medicine has raised the question of whether individuals—in collaboration with health care professionals in their service—should create life or control death.

Most Americans believe contemporary science provides an institutional perspective that is not susceptible to charges of anti-intellectualism. Thus, the institution of modern science provides the backdrop for the public discourse about life, death, and medicine. For instance, federal regulators recently announced that research on "stem cells," extracted from human embryos, did not violate the congressional ban on using federal funds for human embryo research. Stem cells, unlike cells with a specific function such as muscle tissue, have the theoretical capacity to produce all the different types of cells in the human body. The potential application of these types of human stem cells in the treatment of certain diseases such as Parkinson's, Alzheimer's, or juvenile diabetes is simply evidence to proponents of the research that the promise of the Human Genome Project, among other massive scientific inquiries, is being realized.

To opponents of federal participation in human embryo stem cell research, particularly those who also object to abortion, the distinction between the embryo's DNA in its stem cells and its essential humanness sounds like legal hairsplitting. Law in the form of either legislation, regulation, or withholding of federal research support cannot control the social power of the institution of science and its claims of medical progress. Research on human stem cells will continue, despite ethical doubts about the propriety of tinkering with the nature of human life.

Medicine, conjoined with science as an institution, becomes itself an institution upon which history apparently has no impact. The ethical and policy dilemmas of the Tuskegee Syphilis Study and human radiation experiments (1944–1974) are echoed in the present controversy over some types of clinical research performed in hospitals for veterans. The Department of Veterans Affairs recently suspended all research at a Los Angeles veterans' facility for its lack of compliance with federal regulations regarding the obtaining of consent from psychiatric patients for experimental treatments. After this announcement, the local newspaper reported similar lapses at the Los Angeles facility regarding the consent of cardiac patients.[2] At a congressional hearing in the aftermath of this first-time-ever suspension of research at a Veterans Affairs facility, a member of Congress first praised the Department of Veterans Affairs for its leadership in clinical research and its role in creating new treatments, then raised questions about the ethics of conducting experiments on those who have access to no other health care and are quite often members of minority groups.

It should not come as a surprise that dominance of research as an institutional feature of medicine leads inevitably to physician-scientists conducting experiments on patients without their "consent." The choice of regulation and commissions as the method of publicly resolving the ethical dilemmas of biomedical research ensures the continuation of research as a dominant feature of modern medicine, even in those organizational settings most under the control of the federal government.

But the institutional power of science is, in some ways, countered by other institutions, both natural and constructed. Proponents of a ban on human cloning should, according to the analysis in this book, lose those legislative and regulatory battles because of the institutional significance of the family in our democracy. Whatever "family" is or may signify, society cannot—and I will argue it should not—attempt to provide a legal characterization of the family by enacting a statute with one common definition. Rather, "family" as designated in specific legal settings, should have limited purposes: to define, for instance, who is economically responsible for children following divorce or separation of parents; or who should receive government benefits. Furthermore, family as I define it, with at least one parent willing and able to care for a child, takes on many shapes and varieties in our society. Constitutional doctrine provides some limited protection of this diversity of family construction and formation. The majority in any state is thus constrained in its ability to impose its version of the family through legislative action on those who dissent from the nuclear family model or any other model prevailing in that political jurisdiction.

In attempting to define the family legally, one first learns that there is very little regulation of reproductive technologies because, in the American form of democracy, there are many varieties of families. Ironically, this constitutional protection allows "market forces"—the desires of individuals and professionals—to determine whether technology should be used to assist in the birth of a child. Even though the prospect of human cloning makes some of the legal advocates for constitutional protection of reproductive technology uneasy,[3] there is no evidence to suggest that law can overpower the institutional forces that lead individuals to want to form families so long as the technological means exist. A variety of families means that we will have a diversity among communities which will not always coincide with geographical entities such as a state or a territory.[4]

The second, more important lesson is that the constitutional protection of a woman's "right" to terminate a pregnancy should be grounded in theories of family formation, not simply in theories of liberty and the accompanying judicial balancing advocated by "rights theorists" for mediating biomedical dilemmas. Families by their nature, and sometimes by nature aided through technology, are complex; their meanings differ for individuals. To understand why human cloning is not likely to become widespread if left unregulated requires a comparative institutional analysis of the relative importance of families, science, medicine, and law in constructing social meaning for individuals.

A comparative institutional analysis is exactly what individual judges make in forming their opinions. As we consider the question of whether there is a constitutional right to die, we must remember that several years before the debate began over a constitutional right to physician-assisted suicide, the justices had already answered "no." The fact that even so-called "conservative" justices within the institutional constraints of the United States Supreme Court used different methods of reasoning to arrive at their respective "no"s, is an indication that judges have different conceptions of the Court's role in institutional life. This is evident from the different questions each raises about the relationship of legal institutions to the institution of medicine. Underlying all of the justices' questions is a fundamental assumption that legislatures, as opposed to courts, are the primary forum for determining the degree of legal control there should be over modern medicine.

Legislatures provide a process that adjudication cannot. The question about dying that legislatures at the state level have consistently addressed over the past twenty-five years is whether a patient is "terminal." Through court-developed doctrine and legislative ratification, nearly every state has in place the legal means of removing or withholding medical treatment from "terminal" patients with few, if any, possible adverse legal ramifications to physicians. During recent years, however, Dr. Jack Kevorkian, with the help of national media attention, has transformed the public question about the terminally ill by assisting in the death of many patients whom most of us would categorize as "chronically ill." There is, in fact, no legal or legislative definition of "chronically ill," but Kevorkian's gerrymandering rhetoric has forced us to consider if legal definitions of "terminally ill" will suffice in the medically embedded world in which most of us will die of chronic, as opposed to acute, illnesses.

In contrast to medicine, law in general is relatively slow in adapting to social, economic, and ethical changes. The decade-long battle by Michigan prosecutors to convict Jack Kevorkian for his assistance in more than 130 deaths should remind us what "due process" of law means. Law is a rather clumsy process, constrained in our system by its reliance on the past (what lawyers call "precedents") and some traditions (such as the requirement of proof beyond a reasonable doubt) before lay jurors are authorized to convict anyone of a crime. Individuals with resources to acquire lawyers and garner media attention, like Kevorkian, can take advantage of "technicalities" in the pure novelty of the issues they present. Kevorkian's ability to escape conviction for so many years must be seen against the backdrop that application of criminal laws to modern physicians is already fraught with uncertainty. In dealing with the withdrawal or withholding of treatment, the legislature in Michigan and elsewhere has been vigilant in protecting physicians from legal liability for their acts. In others words, physicians in fact run less risk of criminal conviction than most defendants charged with crimes of homicide.[5] The institution of medicine has begun to play an important part in our construct of death. It should come as no surprise that lay jurors had difficulty convicting Kevorkian until prosecutors had new tools—new laws regarding assisted suicide; technological evidence, such as the videotape of Kevorkian injecting a patient; more control over the admissible evidence; and perhaps a shift in public attitudes after the defeat of the initiative to legalize physician-assisted suicide. In any event, convicting a physician, even a defrocked one, for his alleged acts of mercy that symbolize the idea of medical and social progress is a very difficult task for a jury consisting of past and future patients.

As we move into legislative debates about assisted suicide and adequate pain medication, we are reminded that law is itself a complex institution of courts, administrative bodies, commissions, and legislatures. We are now in the legislative era in which acrimony over "rights" in the abortion debate must be replaced by a public discourse that respects our enormous and rich diversity. Although the religious conviction that life begins at conception quite properly did not prevail in the constitutional debate over abortion, it does not mean that the spiritual-ethical and religious position on assisted suicide and euthanasia—that suffering is a necessary part of human life—must be silenced in the legislative and regulatory debates on assisting death. Religion as an institution plays too important a role in American life to be ignored in the public debate over suffering that Drs. Timothy Quill and Jack Kevorkian have forced upon us.

What Quill and Kevorkian offer are secular understandings of suffering which must compete in the legislative debates with a variety of religious perceptions. The institutional analysis proposed in this book helps to explain what many see as a paradox in American politics. In polls, Americans express favorable views towards legalizing some form of physician-assisted death; but they often vote against such proposals, as the 1998 Michigan consensus overwhelmingly indicates. While some legal scholars suggest that church groups' assistance in defeating proposals to legalize physician-assisted suicide is somehow illegitimate or leads to voter irrationality,[6] these views are grounded in a vision of law as solely that of court-developed constitutional doctrine. Within institutional analysis, it is impossible to remove the influence of religious beliefs from voter behavior because those beliefs are intimately tied to individual conceptions of family and community.

When Dr. Quill took his secular crusade for legal immunity in assisting the death of some of his patients to the United States Supreme Court, the Court gave an institutional response: If physicians are to have legal immunity for death-assisting activities, legislatures rather than courts must grant that immunity. While the justices were divided on how they reasoned to that result, they posed more general questions for medicine and those who seek to regulate health care professionals: Should we view physicians as relievers and managers of pain, as determined scientifically rather than existentially? Should we, in our public debates, reject the metaphor of "physicians as relievers of suffering," just as we rejected a previous generation's metaphor of physicians as the preservers of life and the fighters against death? The pain reliever metaphor encourages us to use all of our institutional resources—science, medicine, law, family, and even religion—to assist those with the pain of chronic conditions or terminal illnesses to live and die well.

The United States Supreme Court's opinions on assisted suicide affirmed the right of any state to legalize assisted suicide, and thus retroactively confirmed the constitutionality of the Oregon Death With Dignity Act. The problem remains whether Oregon provides the appropriate direction for other states that might consider the question. I will argue that Oregon is not the model, once we understand that legislatures are the appropriate forum; and the rules of engagement for legislative change are very different from the rights-oriented discussions of the past. Legislative change is a complex process because medicine is already highly regulated by a combination of statutes, court decisions, and administrative regulations. Proponents of the Oregon approach will use a combination of personal tales of horrible deaths and data about the Oregon experience to argue for legislative change.[7] My own prediction is that we will continue to agonize over the role of physicians in our dying, but that very few states will follow the Oregon example. There are many forces within the institution of medicine for limiting the widespread use of lethal doses of drugs even in Oregon, not the least of which is the question of whether pharmacists are willing or ethically bound to fill the prescriptions.[8]

Furthermore, once we recognize that legislatures are the appropriate forum for exercising social control over medicine, it is apparent that the rights view of the relationship of medicine to law is simplistic. For instance, to change the "law" in Michigan to allow physician-assisted death required voters to read and understand a 12,000-word document proposing many modifications of statutes rather than a simple yes or no vote on a slogan about rights. Not surprisingly, at the margin, Michigan citizens voted against the changes in the "law," since the ramifications of those changes to important concepts of family and a sense of connectedness through death were unclear.

The essential problem, as the constitutional debate over physician-assisted suicide has illustrated, is that we cannot deal with death without talking about life. That debate has also demonstrated the limitations of both law and medicine to provide any of us with the choices that lead to meaningful lives and peaceful deaths. What we must seek from both institutions is a matrix that supports choice as well as responsibility for individuals.

For law, that means physicians need both constraints and privileges. Laws prohibiting assisting death are examples of the former, and statutes providing legal immunity for withdrawing life-supporting medical devices are examples of the latter. For medicine, a matrix of choice means that problems of access to health care must be addressed. Whether patients get the pain medication they need is simply a microcosm of the much larger problem of how the system of education, training, and financing health care leaves many in our society without effective access to physicians, who are "gatekeepers" for the vast majority of us who will be in some system of managed care. With effective leadership, however, the matrix of choice for health care is different from, say, the matrix of choice between purchasing a Honda or a Chevrolet. There are vast personal, social, and ethical issues involved in how we live and die.

A political alliance between physicians and present, past, and future patients is easy to build because of the institutional force of medicine. The current popularity of the idea that patients need "rights" to cope with the new form of health care delivery called "managed care" reinforces the centrality of the physician-patient dyad. Legislation that tries, for example, to ensure a mother's "right" to forty-eight hours of hospital stay after delivery of a child masks much deeper problems of public policy. For instance, should physicians be the leaders in proposing some system of providing health care for pregnant women and newborns? What might physicians, working in collaboration with insurance groups and governments, devise that might provide a model in one state? Would such a coalition be able to appeal to our own sense of obligation of self-care to help us see that "free" health care for some pregnant women might in fact be cost-effective in the long run?

In a democratic and pluralistic society, many of these questions will have to involve political processes, with all of their limitations. Eventually, physicians themselves will have to propose some alternatives to our present crisis approach to cost containment and reasonable access to health care. Medicine and law are social systems within a dynamic, fluid community. Neither medicine nor law can provide meaningful lives or graceful deaths, but these social systems can provide choices that affirm for individuals who they are. It is within this matrix of choice that beginnings as well as endings have value for each of us, as well as for our society.

NOTES

1. Stephen L. Carter, *The Dissent of the Governed: A Meditation on Law, Religion, and Loyalty* (Cambridge, MA: Harvard University Press, 1998), 142.

2. *Los Angeles Times*, March 25, 1999, p. 1.

3. Lori B. Andrews, *The Clone Age: Adventures in the New World of Reproductive Technology* (New York: Henry Holt and Company, 1999), 260.

4. Carter, *The Dissent of the Governed*, 26, 55.

5. Larry I. Palmer, *Law, Medicine and Social Justice* (Louisville, KY: Westminster/John Knox Press, 1989), 94–107.

6. Ronald Dworkin, *Life's Dominion: An Argument about Abortion, Euthanasia, and Individual Freedom* (New York: Vantage Books, 1994), 4.

7. Arthur E. Chin et al., "Legalized Physician-Assisted Suicide in Oregon—The First Year's Experience," *New England Journal of Medicine* 340 (February 18, 1999): 577–83.

8. "Board of Directors Report on the Council on Legal and Public Affairs," *American Journal of Health System Pharmacists* 56 (1999): 652–59.

PART I
THE ROLE OF LAW IN OUR INTIMATE LIVES

Chapter 1

Science in the Service of Medicine and Law

Doctors . . . are applied scientists.

Lewis Thomas[1]

Americans share an ideology of the social function of medicine: a belief about the necessity of linking the practice of medicine to modern science, with all the social benefits and risks inherent in this institutional alliance. This powerful union makes innovation—the constant search for more effective treatments—the hallmark or "icon" of modern medicine. Several examples come to mind. The Tuskegee Study of Untreated Syphilis in the Negro Male—a dark chapter in our medical and public health history—has enduring significance for public policy debates. Our government's sponsorship of the Human Genome Project—a massive scientific and technological effort to discover the individual structures of the thousands of genes in the human species—demonstrates how the social role of science in the service of medicine has been institutionalized. Finally, the recent revelations in a government-appointed advisory group's report that perhaps thousands of individuals unknowingly took part in human radiation experiments after World War II dictate a reexamination of the actual meaning of supposed requirements of "informed consent" ethics and practices of American physicians and scientists.

TUSKEGEE: A CASE OF GOOD PEOPLE, BAD
INSTITUTIONAL ARRANGEMENTS

The Tuskegee Study of Untreated Syphilis in the Negro Male was a forty-year study (1932–1972) conducted by the United States Public Health Service to document the long-term effects of syphilis. The study tracked some 400 men from Macon County, Alabama, by charting their health via annual medical exams and by performing autopsies on the more than 100 men who died over the course of the study. The men were never told that they were subjects of a study, nor were they ever told the exact nature of their disease.[2]

A variety of professionals participated to create this bleak period in our medical history. Physicians employed by the United States Public Health Service, and later physicians and scientists at the Centers for Disease Control (CDC), were significant actors in the ongoing study over the forty-year period. Physicians within the Macon County area "referred" those African Americans who sought treatment for their syphilis to the government physicians. Public Health nurses kept track of the subjects and assisted in arranging their annual checkups, as well as the autopsies and burials of those who died.[3] Thus, the existence of the study was no secret, at least to the readers of professional journals on infectious diseases and the medical professionals in Macon County.[4]

After the revelations of the Tuskegee Study, Congress enacted, and the president signed, the National Research Act of 1974, which established a commission to study the ethical principles that should govern the use of human subjects in biomedical and behavioral research.[5] Congress gave the commissioners a very broad mandate and some specific charges, asking, for instance, for a report on the use of "psychosurgery" in the United States.[6] The commission was also instructed to identify the relationship of the "requirements for informed consent" to research.[7] "Commissioning ethics"—periodic appointment of multidisciplinary groups to make reports about ethical issues related to medicine—has become a permanent feature of public discussions about the ethical dilemmas created by modern medicine.[8]

The act also authorized the then Department of Health, Education, and Welfare (HEW) to issue regulations governing federally funded research.[9] The pillar of the system of regulation established by HEW was the "institutional review board"—a committee of individuals within the hospital, university, or research center—and its supposed capacity to supervise the taking of consent. The board would assist the investigator in cost-benefit analysis in deciding whether the use of human subjects was appropriate in any specific research project. Without this institutional assurance, federal funds for research should be denied. The current regulations governing research sponsored by federal agencies evolved from the authority granted to HEW by the 1974 act.[10]

Congress's explicit delegation of the scope of regulation of research to an administrative agency and the establishment of a high profile commission represents a political compromise that is inherent in the legislative process. On the one hand, there is public acknowledgment that some professionals acted unethically during the Tuskegee Study and other such projects in the 1960s and 1970s. On the other hand, the benefits of modern medicine appear to have come from trusting individual investigators' initiatives and individual dedication to serving the public good. Physicians, like other special interest groups, have the ability to communicate their concerns to members of Congress, pointing out the potential risks to their professional decision making of legal intervention into their activities.[11] Under this assumption, a new criminal statute regarding improper human experimentation—one theoretical legislative option—would be seen as inhibiting physicians' and scientists' initiative.

Yet doing nothing in response to the history of professional abuses apparent in Tuskegee and other events of the 1960s and 1970s was politically unacceptable. For any piece of legislation to get passed by Congress, it must mediate between the interests of physician/investigator autonomy and those who believe that direct legal controls over physician decision making is the only way of preventing future Tuskegees. The National Research Act represents just such a compromise between those two competing political forces. The result: some political action, but little actual legal oversight of physicians or scientists through the administrative process.

The dominance of administrative decision making in human research in this country represents a public policy choice that seeks the appropriate balance between the science/medicine alliance and those social institutions that might inhibit the basic thrust of innovation and the promise of more effective health care. The inability of a legislature to provide a definitive answer to: What can we do to prevent another Tuskegee? is emblematic of the power of medicine when linked with the institution of science in our times.

The Tuskegee Study left another legal legacy, that of compensation by settlement. Fred Gray, who had a long history of involvement with civil rights litigation,[12] was the lead attorney representing the plaintiffs in the 1973 class action lawsuit for monetary damages. With the assistance of lawyers from the NAACP Legal Defense Fund, he filed suit against the United States, government officials in what was then HEW, the state of Alabama, a private foundation, and individual physicians working for the United States Public Health Service.

The complaint asked the Federal District Court to declare that the defendants' conduct violated the constitutional rights of the survivors and the deceased participants. It also asked that each survivor or decedent representative be awarded $1.5 million as compensation for the "deprivation" of their constitutional rights.[13] After numerous pretrial maneuvers, the lawyers for the plaintiffs and the United States government reached a monetary settlement in which each living survivor received $37,500, each heir or representative of a deceased subject received $15,000, each of the "controls" received $16,000, and each heir or representative of a control received $5,000 from the $10 million settlement that the federal government paid.[14]

Gray's legal theory in the suit for damages was that the tenant farmers were selected by the Public Health Service for the study solely because they were African Americans.[15] As a consequence, he did not name as possible defendants any of the African American physicians or nurses involved in the study.[16] Under Gray's conception, their legal culpability was mitigated by their victimization through a racially segregated medical profession and society. Accordingly, race had greater explanatory force than notions of professionalism—which might have influenced both the Caucasian and African American professionals over the forty-year period of the study.

A lawsuit seeking monetary damages for allegedly inappropriate actions of professionals is one—though not totally effective—means of retrospective social control over physicians and scientists. The lesson in this "compensation by settlement" is that lawyers, trained to think of adjudication, are not always "reflective practitioners."[17] Lawyers crafting settlements and drafting legislation in the aftermath of the public outrage over the Tuskegee Study may have operated without an institutional conception of law in relationship to modern science and medicine.[18]

Finally, the Tuskegee Study has left a political legacy. David Feldshuh's highly acclaimed 1989 play based on the Tuskegee Study, *Miss Evers' Boys*, and the 1997 HBO movie adaptation of the play have increased public awareness of the ethical legacy of the study. In May 1997, three months after HBO's airing of its version of *Miss Evers' Boys*, President Clinton, on behalf of the United States, apologized for the Tuskegee Study in a televised White House ceremony. After being introduced by one of the eight survivors, President Clinton declared, "The United States government did something that was wrong—deeply, profoundly, morally wrong . . . on behalf of the American people what the United States government did was shameful and I am sorry."[19] While the newscaster focused on the high drama and emotion of the White House ceremony, consider the short and long-term institutional consequences. In the short term, President Clinton, in the course of his remarks, announced a federal grant to the Tuskegee Institute to plan a center on bioethics and health care, ordered the secretary of health and human services to issue a report on how to involve minority communities in research on improving health care, and announced increased federal efforts to advance the training of African Americans as bioethicists.

In the long term, Clinton's apology and allocation of federal funds has institutionalized the Tuskegee Study in two ways. First, the political apology effectively ends the ethical debate about how the researchers are to be judged. Their conduct is not to be evaluated by the medical profession's ethics of 1932. Rather, the physician or physician/scientist in Tuskegee will be judged in hindsight by evolving standards of the appropriate institutional balance between science, medicine, and law, which cannot be codified in advance.[20] Second, the allocation of funds simultaneous with the apology provided an opportunity for the president to put his imprimatur on the efforts to increase the number of members of minority groups involved in federally sponsored research projects. Clinton's attempt to "integrate" both the bioethics profession and the pool of individuals participating in federally sponsored research implies, ironically, very little legal control over research or science.

The Tuskegee Study is a reminder that when medicine pushes the frontiers, legal responses in terms of alleged constitutional rights do not necessarily bring viable solutions or help devise the best institutional arrangements among law, medicine, and modern science. Lawyers, like their medical counterparts, are sometimes moved by perceptions that problems and people are susceptible to the expediency that passes for kindness.[21] The professionals involved in the study were in fact "good" individuals, unable to see that they practiced medicine—and later, law—under what were "bad" institutional arrangements.

GENETIC HEALTH AND THE "MAPPING" OF THE HUMAN GENOME

In the early 1970s, some scientists took an unusual step in response to the public's growing awareness of the dangers of scientific research. A group of scientists and some invited guests met to consider whether a certain line of genetic transformation research should "voluntarily" be discontinued until the "risks" of the research could be ascertained.[22] At the time, no actual human beings were subjects of any experiments; rather, this laboratory research sought to understand how genes function to bring about certain results in biological organisms. The conflict over whether "recombinant DNA" research—such as putting a cancer-causing virus that normally lived in monkeys into a bacterium—should continue was resolved through the establishment of federal regulations allowing most research to go forward by 1975.

These regulations classified the risks involved in certain types of experiments and required appropriate containment measures within laboratories to ensure that these technologically altered biological organisms did not escape into the environment or into humans. Over time, the research community was able to convince federal regulators that the risks were not as great as even some of them had once thought, and "bio-technology" and its promise for human medicine (as well as plant and animal science) went forward. Scientists all over the world are now investigating the genetic nature of hundreds of diseases.[23]

Essentially "scientific views" of the human place in the universe often focus on scientific innovation as a panacea. Some social scientists share this vision, which holds that a definable social progress is a higher social good, to be attained by a variety of means which might be inconsistent with humanistic thought.[24] The possible health care benefits of genetic research are now so prominent in public discourse that the complexities of ethical dilemmas inherent in modern scientific research are often ignored. A recent report in the press noting the higher incidence of diabetes among African Americans leads to the speculation that there may be a genetic "cause" of diabetes.[25] An alternative explanation—that the difference is explained by environmental conditions of the fetus, and that there exists a correlation between the fetal environment and the social and economic status of the mothers of many African American children—is almost drowned out of public discourse in the zeal to find the cause of ill health in the genetic make-up of certain individuals.[26]

James Watson, who along with Sir Francis Crick was the codiscoverer of the structure of DNA, convinced the federal government to establish the Human Genome Project in 1988. Watson became the first director of a project that was to oversee the expenditure of billions of dollars in the pursuit of the identity and structure of all the genes of the human species by 2003, the fiftieth anniversary of Watson and Crick's discovery. A large percentage of funds for research available for disbursement by the National Institutes of Health (NIH) and the Department of Energy (DOE) will be expended to fit within the grand design of "mapping" the human genome.[27]

The pursuit of genetic knowledge, however, will take scientists beyond national borders as they seek to determine whether what might be social and geographic differences in disease patterns are in fact genetic differences. Discovering that the higher rate of asthma among an isolated island population might have a genetic "cause" could lead to more effective treatment of asthma among Western populations. But first, the genetic explorers must obtain samples from the non-Western, isolated populations.[28] How, and under what circumstances, physicians and scientists should attempt to obtain these DNA samples raises a host of ethical questions. The use of a population simply to improve health care delivery in Western societies seems hardly appropriate. Physicians and scientists engaged in such genetic "decoding" might have some sense that these isolated and indigenous people ought to be offered "treatment" for their asthma. Such treatment could certainly be viewed as obligatory, or even a moral necessity. But it could also be argued that intrusion into this population's immediate lives, as well as into their medically-altered future, might signal some further response. Once again, the questions multiply as a single answer is sought by medicine.

While the public anticipates medical benefits, individuals worry about the use of genetic knowledge outside the health care delivery system. Given that large employers pay the health costs of their employees, will, at the margin, an employer who knew a potential employee had the "gene" for cancer, instead hire an applicant without that "gene"? The public response so far has been an attempt to prevent "discrimination" on the basis of genetics. For instance, "genetic testing" has now been defined by statute to mean, among other things, "a test of a person's genes, gene products or chromosomes," and insurance providers and employers are prohibited from using genetic testing in a discriminatory manner.[29]

But the specter of genetic information as power creates concerns outside of law. The "discovery" that the incidence of some forms of breast cancer is greater among women of eastern European Jewish ancestry could, for example, lead to "overtreatment" of these women.[30] When concerns like these are raised, even scientists admit that the eugenics movement in the 1920s and 1930s in Germany and Europe had its American counterparts, which resulted in legislation restricting the immigration of many of the individuals who subsequently died in Nazi concentration camps.[31]

THE HUMAN RADIATION EXPERIMENTS:
A CASE OF INSTITUTIONAL FAILURE

Until the issuance of *The Final Report of the Advisory Committee on Human Radiation Experiments* in October 1995, the general public had no official acknowledgment that our national government had sponsored thousands of experiments to test the effects of radiation on humans. As the committee members and staff attempted to convey the story of how scientists and physicians working in various government agencies, hospitals, universities, and research centers around the country for many years conducted these experiments, the committee had to confront the meaning of the Nuremberg Judgment for American professionals.

Despite the fact that the American Medical Association adopted the Nuremberg Code regarding the necessity of informed consent in experimental and therapeutic settings, the committee's own interviews revealed that in practice the rules regarding the necessity of consent were not strictly adhered to by professionals in a variety of research settings.[32] Among the many findings in the nearly thousand-page report, the committee detailed what had been widely speculated in the media for many years:

- From 1944 to 1974, the federal government sponsored several thousand human radiation experiments, some of which were to advance medical knowledge and others to promote the government's interest in strengthening the military or its space exploration program.

- From these experiments, clinical researchers developed new therapies such as the use of radioactive iodine to treat thyroid cancer and methods of identifying tumors.[33]

- The federal government did not have a comprehensive policy on consent of all subjects of research until 1974.[34]

- Some American military service personnel were used in experiments in connection with the testing of atomic bombs.[35]

- After the end of the Manhattan Project in 1946, many government-sponsored human experiments were kept secret without any official classification as such, out of concern about embarrassing the government, legal liability, or perceptions about possible public misunderstanding of the necessity of human research.[36]

- The government agencies sponsoring these various experiments did not routinely create records that would allow those who came later with questions to evaluate the propriety of those experiments.[37]

It would be comforting to find evil motives, bad education, or a paucity of ethics among the individual participants. Too many physicians, scientists, and researchers in the many different organizational settings worked long and hard—and in some cases, well. What all these scientists and physicians had in common was an assumption about "medical progress." Within that supposition was the further belief that professionals are ethically justified in inflicting some individual patient suffering, or even death, in order to achieve a greater social good for future patients, some of whom might be injured military personnel.

The human radiation experiments' narrative is an example of institutional failure on a grand scale. The government officials sponsoring the radiation experiments *assumed* that scientists and physicians would act in accordance with prevailing ethical standards. Physicians and scientists *assumed* without question that their practices of not informing patients were not in violation of the Nuremberg Code, since the known risks of death from the experiments were small and the United States government officials had decided that such experiments were in the national interest. University officials signing government contracts to conduct "secret" research *had confidence* in the research scientists to make judgments about the appropriateness of the research in advancing knowledge. None of these individuals had been trained to pose and confront the public policy problem of human experimentation: Which institutional processes are most likely to help society arrive at the optimal amount of human experimentation?

ADJUDICATION AND THE NUREMBERG CODE

The total-body radiation experiments at the University of Cincinnati College of Medicine illustrate the institutional dilemma. From 1960 until 1972, the United States Department of Defense sponsored research to determine the effect of radiation on eighty-seven patients with cancer at Cincinnati General Hospital. The military purpose of this cold war research was to gather more information on the level of radiation human beings could endure and to find "a biological dosimeter."[38]

What the patients—all with serious forms of cancer—and their family members were told remains in dispute. It is apparent that the purpose of this research changed over time, as funding sources and public knowledge of and interest in the total-body radiation experiments fluctuated. At one point, after a public outcry, the researchers at the University of Cincinnati Medical College stated in professional journals that the purpose of the research was to improve the clinical treatment and management of patients with advanced cancer. But when reporting on the research to the military sponsors during the early years of the project, the researchers emphasized the importance of understanding the effects of radiation on humans.[39]

Two features about the Cincinnati story remain undisputed. First, the University of Cincinnati was simply the last of several academically distinguished institutions which had assisted in the government's desire to understand the effects of radiation should there be a nuclear strike on the United States or its military personnel. The University of Rochester, Baylor University College of Medicine, Memorial Sloan-Kettering Institute for Cancer Research, and the United States Naval Hospital are among the other organizations that received funds to study the effects of total-body radiation over the years.[40] Second, all the congressional investigations, books, media focus, and advisory committee analyses of the Cincinnati studies over the past twenty-five years have not told the complete story of the social dilemma these experiments generated.

When a newspaper reporter announced the identity of these subjects for the first time in November 1993,[41] it was perhaps inevitable that a lawsuit would follow. The relatives of the cancer patients in the University of Cincinnati General Hospital study filed a lawsuit against the physicians, the University of Cincinnati, the government officials supervising the study for the Department of Defense, and the city of Cincinnati. In the lawsuit, the plaintiffs claimed their long-dead relatives were not told the purposes of the total-body radiation, and in fact had been told that the radiation was a treatment for their advanced cancers. As a result, the patients did not receive the appropriate care for their cancers, or perhaps more important, care for their dying, which they would have received had their treating physicians not been participants in a secret military study on the effects of human radiation.[42]

The defendants took the position that there were no legal grounds for recovery of any monetary damages and filed a motion to dismiss the lawsuit. This motion, if successful, would have prevented the plaintiffs from presenting any evidence about events over twenty-five years ago. The trial judge assigned to hear the case has denied the individual defendants' motion and allowed the lawsuit to proceed.[43]

In the course of rendering his opinion, the trial judge attempted to place the lawsuit in its historical context by making use of the Nuremberg Code to bolster its reasoning. The judge implied that a 1953 memorandum regarding research made the officials in the Department of Defense and the physicians at the University of Cincinnati aware that the research project should have conformed to the Nuremberg Code on obtaining the consent of research subjects. This memorandum from the secretary of defense to the secretaries of the army, navy, and air force ordered that the code be followed in all military-sponsored research. As a consequence, the court reasoned that the prevailing practice among professionals in 1960 would have required the defendants to obtain "informed consent" from the patients.

The trial judge did not, however, provide us with the relevant social and historical context of the issuance of the 1953 memorandum. It was classified as "top secret" until 1975.[44] And there is no evidence that the physicians at the University of Cincinnati had any knowledge of the memorandum. Since their experiments were on patients they considered terminal, it is not as clear as the court suggests that these physicians would or should have understood that the Nuremberg Code applied in clinical settings. The Advisory Committee's Oral Ethics Project suggests that when American researchers were studying patients, consent for research was not always sought, since obtaining consent for all treatments was not the norm.[45] It is significant that the judge assumed that the Nuremberg medical experiment ruling announcing the code is the defining event in the relationship of law, science, medicine, and the military.

This ruling created the possibility that events surrounding the Cincinnati studies would be reconstructed using the rules of evidence for a jury, and, adjudication would have become the means by which this alliance of government, universities, and scientists in pursuit of medical progress might have been given a human face through the stories the plaintiffs told. However, after over two years of protracted negotiations, the lawsuit was settled, with most of the families receiving about $50,000 each and without solutions that eliminate the possibility of improper human experimentation. As the litigation in the aftermath of the Tuskegee Study demonstrates, the law alone offers just another prismatic view, and produces more questions.

The Advisory Committee seemed to realize that it had raised a large number of questions, both public and private.[46] The authors of the report candidly admit that among the hundreds of individuals with whom the committee members and staff spoke, the most commonly asked question was: How can I find out if I or my relative was in a radiation experiment?[47] The correct answer to that question is the hardest for a modern professional to give: I don't know. Leaving a written narrative of how to continue individual personal or scholarly quests, the Advisory Committee's report concludes with an appendix, "A Citizen's Guide to the Nation's Archives: Where the Records Are and How to Find Them."[48]

The committee also left a very modern legacy—databases of information related to the radiation experiments that are available through various sites on the Internet. With so much data so widely available, one might suppose a thorough understanding of the social forces generating the human radiation experiments. However, until the public abandons the notion that these social and ethical dilemmas are simply the legacy of bad professionals, scholars will not develop the types of institutional analyses that allow a sifting through of the data to arrive at social solutions.

CONCLUSION

Americans have accepted human research as a necessary part of social life. They have faith in the idea of medical progress. Periodic legal intervention into human research in the form of lawsuits, commissions on medical ethics, and legislation are all correctives to the abuses they believe are simply a matter of a few "bad individuals." But the physician-patient dyad cannot remain the center of ethical analysis. That true center is the larger social question: Which moral paradigms will governments, insurers, health care providers, and employers use in the future in designing systems of physician-patient interaction?[49]

The relatives of the now-dead cancer patients in the Cincinnati General Hospital study are reminders that the legal claims of the lack of "informed consent" are, at bottom, after-the-fact allegations of inappropriate care. In this case, if the plaintiffs can convince a jury of their perspectives, there will be a judgment that the physicians mistakenly treated dying human beings as if they were nothing more than protoplasm in petri dishes. A court is willing to entertain such a lawsuit because law embodies a form of remembered human connection.

Modern medical research, particularly in its search for the genetic understanding of health and disease, has heightened the ability of professionals to "play the God game" because of patient "faith" in medical progress.[50] The regulatory processes developed over the past twenty years to deal with human experimentation have at the same time increased the amount of these experiments, as well as the growth of new cures and greater life expectancy. There is also the concomitant growth in the possibility for individual pain and suffering. Perhaps nothing so nakedly shocking as the Tuskegee Study would happen now, but other events are happening and will happen. This is why institutional analysis is so critical. In the face of this powerful cultural alliance between science and medicine, legal institutions must intervene in ways that maximize the likelihood that individual notions of death, decay, and health will prevail over professional notions of medical progress.

NOTES

1. Lewis Thomas, *The Youngest Science: Notes of a Medicine-Watcher* (New York: Bantam Books, 1984), 54.

2. Larry I. Palmer, *Study Guide for Discussion Leaders, Susceptible to Kindness*: *Miss Evers' Boys and the Tuskegee Syphilis Study* (Ithaca, NY: Cornell University, 1994), 8. For a detailed account of the study, see James H. Jones, *Bad Blood: The Tuskegee Syphilis Experiment* (New York: Free Press, 1993). What the Tuskegee Study of Untreated Syphilis in the Negro Male *was* creates some controversy in the context of the physician-assisted suicide debate. For instance, Jack Kevorkian, a longtime advocate of using death row prisoners for medical experiments, has stated that the Tuskegee Study involved imprisoned black inmates. See Kevorkian, *Prescription Medicide: The Goodness of Planned Death* (Buffalo, NY: Prometheus Books, 1991), 170.

3. Jones, *Bad Blood*, 151–55.

4. Several articles discussing the study appeared in various medical journals, including R. A. Vonderlehr et al., "Untreated Syphilis in the Male Negro: A Comparative Study of Treated and Untreated Cases," *Venereal Disease Information* 17 (1936): 260–65; Sidney Olansky et al., "Environmental Factors in the Tuskegee Study of Untreated Syphilis," *Public Health Reports* 69 (1954): 691–98; Donald H. Rockwell et al., "The Tuskegee Study of Untreated Syphilis: The 30th Year of Observation," *Archives of Internal Medicine* 114 (1961): 792–98; as well as ten other published reports. See generally Jones, *Bad Blood*, 281–82.

5. National Research Act of 1974 § 2029(a)(1)(C), Pub. L. No. 93–348, 88 Stat. 348 (codified as amended in 42 U.S.C. § 289*l*-1).

6. "The Commission shall conduct an investigation and study of the use of psychosurgery in the United States during the five-year period ending December 31, 1972." National Research Act, § 202(c).

7. National Research Act, § 202(a)(1)(A).

8. David J. Rothman, *Strangers at the Bedside: A History of How Law and Bioethics Transformed Medical Decisionmaking* (New York: Basic Books, 1991), 255.

9. National Research Act at § 212, 88 Stat. at 352–53 (codified as amended in 42 U.S.C. § 289*l*-3).

10. *Final Report of the Advisory Committee on Human Radiation Experiments* (Washington, DC: GPO, 1995), 671. Note that the regulations also cover research at institutions receiving federal grant support. Thus, all university-sponsored research is covered by these regulations, but not necessarily research carried out by private companies who receive no government support. Nor do the regulations cover research conducted by United States citizens outside of the United States.

11. Neil K. Komesar, *Imperfect Alternatives: Choosing Institutions in Law, Economics, and Public Policy* (Chicago: University of Chicago Press, 1994), 54–65, 115–21.

12. Most notably as the lawyer who represented Rosa Parks of the Montgomery Bus Boycott in 1955, *Parks v. City of Montgomery*, 38 Ala. App. 681 (1957). See Jones, *Bad Blood*, 212.

13. Plantiff's Complaint, *Pollard v. United States* (M.D. Ala. 1973) (No. 4126-N). Complaint at 12–13. This is thus a lawsuit seeking damages for deprivation of rights under color of law under 18 U.S.C. § 1983. This one statute has created a body of law, the significance of which I do not deal with here.

14. Jones, *Bad Blood*, 217.

15. ¶ 13 of the complaint states: "The subjects of the study were racially selected: only black men were used as subjects in the study. . . . Plaintiffs allege that the black subjects were selected and used in the experiment, a program of controlled genocide solely because of their race and color in violation of their rights, secured by the Constitution and Laws of the United States." Plaintiff's Complaint, *Pollard v. United States* at 10–11.

16. James Jones states:

The Tuskegee Institute, for which Gray served as the general counsel, was not named in the suit. Neither was the Veteran's Hospital. The local hospital and the Macon County Medical Society also escaped legal notice. In fact, no predominantly black institution was named in the suit. The same was true of all individuals: all of the individually named defendants were white. No black physicians were mentioned; neither were any black nurses.

Jones, *Bad Blood*, 216.

17. See generally Donald Schön, *The Reflective Practitioner: How Professionals Think in Action* (New York: Basic Books, 1983).

18. See generally Larry I. Palmer, "Life, Death, and Public Policy." Review of *Imperfect Alternatives: Choosing Institutions in Law, Economics, and Public Policy*, by Neil K. Komesar. *Cornell Law Review* 81 (1995): 161–80.

19. *World News Morning*, "Bill Clinton to Apologize for Tuskegee Experiment—Victims and Families in Washington for Apology" (CNN television broadcast May 16, 1997). See also transcript, note 25.

20. Jeffrey J. Rachlinski, "A Positive Psychological Theory of Judging in Hindsight," *University of Chicago Law Review* 65 (1998): 571–625.

21. Twenty years after Tuskegee became the subject of media stories and scholarly works, David Feldshuh recreated the professional and ethical dilemmas of the infamous study through his prize-winning play, *Miss Evers' Boys*. The main protagonist of his play is Nurse Eunice Evers, an African American public health nurse who is employed to track the men in the study and act as the liaison

between the physicians and their patient-subjects. The other characters in the play are Dr. Eugene Brodus, the African American administrator of a hospital serving African Americans in Tuskegee; Dr. John Douglas, a Caucasian field physician in the United States Public Health Service; and four African American tenant farmers.

The inner conflict in Nurse Evers, the heroine with whom we identify, grows throughout the play as she carries out the physicians' orders to deceive the men into believing they were receiving treatment when in reality they were subjects of a study of untreated disease. The development of her inner moral conflict about her relationship with the men is what gives the play its tragic nature. In the epilogue to the play, Miss Evers is testifying before the United States Senate Committee considering legislation concerning research with human subjects. Justifying her role in the forty-year study, she declares: "I . . . loved those men . . . they were susceptible to kindness."

See *Miss Evers' Boys* (Home Box Office, 1997). President Clinton, Remarks in Apology for Tuskegee Story (May 16, 1997). (Transcript available from U.S. Newswire on Lexis-Nexis) [hereinafter Transcript]. See also Larry I. Palmer, "Paying for Suffering: The Problem of Human Experimentation," *Maryland Law Review* 56 (1998): 604–23.

22. During the Asilomar Conference, February 24–27, 1975, 139 molecular biologists from seventeen nations approved guidelines for reducing the experimental risks of gene-grafting research. The conference was called by a committee of U.S. biologists who feared such experimentation might accidentally produce drug-resistant or carcinogenic organisms. "Gene-Grafting Research Guidelines Set," *Facts on File World News Digest* (April 19, 1975): sec. miscellaneous. See also Judith Areen et al., *Law, Science, and Medicine* (Mineola, NY: Foundation Press, 1984), 12–44.

23. Robert Pollack, *Signs of Life: The Language and Meaning of DNA* (New York: Houghton Mifflin Company, 1994).

24. Sir Francis Crick, the codiscoverer of the structure of DNA, asserted that children should not receive religious instruction because it would inhibit their acquiring the scientific view of man's place in the universe and the nature of scientific truth. In addition, Crick suggested that parents of identical twins should be permitted to dedicate one of them to society so the two siblings could be raised in different environments and compared. While Crick's social views might be extreme, his vision that innovation in science leads to social progress is widely shared by scientists and laymen alike. Robert Pollack, *Signs of Life*, 62–63 (quoting News Item, "Logic of Biology," *Nature* 220 [1968]: 429–30).

25. There have been great advances in the health benefits of understanding the genetic nature of disease processes, such as in diabetes research which has produced genetically engineered human insulin. But as Robert Pollack points out:

In the absence of clear legal boundaries, we are at risk of developing a de facto national eugenics policy after all, not because we wish to identify and then eliminate people as undesirable members of 'lesser races,' but because some alleles will be considered undesirable by organizations in a position to limit their replication.

Pollack, *Signs of Life*, 110.
26. Pollack, *Signs of Life*, 9.

27. Pollack, *Signs of Life*, 95–96; Evgeny Zaychikov, "Mapping of Catalytic Residues in the RNA Polymerase Active Center," *Science* 273 (July 5, 1996): 107–9. This does not mean that research on the structure of genes in plants or other animals is excluded from the project's funds, since knowledge gained about genetic structure is in some sense transferable across specific species. The "maps" of the chromosomes of the favorite experimental organisms—yeast, fruit fly, roundworm, and mouse are rapidly being sketched in.

28. Patricia Kahn, "Genetic Diversity Project Tries Again," *Science* 266 (1994): 720–22.

29. Wis. Stat. §§ 111.32 (7m), 111.372 (1994).

30. See, for example, Kenneth Offit et al., "Germline BRCA1 185delAG Mutations in Jewish Women with Breast Cancer," *Lancet* 347 (June 15, 1996): 1643–45 and "Cancer Gene has Jewish Connection; A Genetic Test for a Specific Ethnic Group Could Lead to Discrimination, Some Say," *Des Moines Register* (September 29, 1995): 8.

31. Pollack, *Signs of Life*, 7–8, 56–63.

32. See *Final Report of the Advisory Committee on Human Radiation Experiments*, 144–49.

33. Ibid., finding 3, 779.

34. Ibid., finding 4, 780–81.

35. Ibid., finding 12, 789–90.

36. Ibid., finding 15, 791–92.

37. Ibid., finding 19, 794–95.

38. Ibid., 385.

39. Ibid., 387.

40. See chapter 8, "Total-Body Radiation Irradiation," in *Final Report of the Advisory Committee on Human Radiation Experiments*, 366–420.

41. In what later earned her a Pulitzer Prize, reporter Eileen Welsome of the *Albuquerque Tribune* first publicized the existence of the experiments by tracking the case histories of five former subjects in a series of articles in November 1993. She was able to identify these five of the eighteen subjects injected with plutonium with the aid of genealogists, historians, and cemetery employees. Within weeks, the radiation experiments were national news, and other reporters had uncovered the names of two more former subjects. U.S. Congress, House. *Hearings on Energy and Power Federal Government Testing of Human Subjects for Studies of the Effect of Radiation*. Testimony of Eileen Welsome. 103rd Cong., January 18, 1994.

42. *In Re Cincinnati Radiation Litigation*, 874F. Supp. 796, 814 (S.D. Ohio 1995).

43. The protracted process leading to the $4.6 million settlement is described in Tim Bonfield, "Plague Doesn't End Pain: Radiation Controversy Outlasts the Settlement," *The Cincinnati Enquirer*, October 9, 1999.

44. *Final Report of the Advisory Committee on Human Radiation Experiments*, 106. It is highly probable that in the midst of the cold war, the document was classified as secret in order to keep the military's sponsorship of biological and chemical research from the public. It is possible—though I submit highly unlikely—that such a document was widely disseminated to officials in the military's research units during the cold war.

45. Ibid., 161.

46. The *Final Report of the Advisory Committee on Human Radiation Experiments* failed to receive much media attention because it was released to the press on October 3, 1995, the same day Judge Ito asked the jury to reveal O. J. Simpson's fate to the world. President Clinton's press conference on the report followed the announcement of that verdict by thirty minutes. While major newspapers did have some coverage of the report's release, journalists and their readers were, not surprisingly, more interested in the two-word finding of the Simpson jury than the nearly 1,000-page tome of the Advisory Committee.

47. *Final Report of the Advisory Committee on Human Radiation Experiments*, 897.

48. Ibid., 896.

49. Komesar, *Imperfect Alternatives*, 158–61; Einer Elhauge, "Allocating Health Care Morally," *California Law Review* 82 (December, 1994): 1449–544. See also Marjorie Maguire Shultz, "From Informed Consent to Patient Choice: A New Protected Interest," *Yale Law Journal* 95 (1985): 219–99.

50. See generally Rothman, *Strangers at the Bedside*.

_____ Chapter 2 _____

Assisted Reproduction: Do We Need Legislative Definitions of the Family?

Legislative consideration of surrogacy may [also] provide the opportunity to begin to focus on the overall implications of the new reproductive biotechnology—in vitro fertilization, preservation of sperms and eggs, embryo implantation and the like.

In the Matter of Baby M[1]

Assisted reproduction—artificial insemination, in vitro fertilization with or without egg or sperm donation, surrogate parentage, and even human cloning—challenge traditional notions of the family. Over a decade ago, while declaring "surrogate parenting contracts" void and legally unenforceable, the New Jersey Supreme Court suggested that legislatures were better suited than courts for providing comprehensive legal resolutions to the problems of assisted reproduction.

A decade later, other appellate courts are still making similar calls for comprehensive legislative solutions while ruling on the disposition of frozen embryos,[2] the enforceability of surrogate parenting contracts,[3] the support obligations to a child without any genetic or gestational connection to the wife or the husband,[4] and the effects of divorce on voluntary surrogate arrangements.[5] Implicit in these judicial calls for legislative solutions is the question: Do we need legislative definitions of the family? So far, no legislature has adopted comprehensive regulation of all forms of assisted reproduction. I propose a very cautious approach when we consider legislative action concerning the family. When the institution of the family is seen as child-centered, new shape is given to individual political priorities. Our elected officials should reject a majoritarian answer as to what constitutes a family. The lack of legislative action on ethically divisive issues means, in effect, that professionals— medical and legal—will have a great deal of influence on whether individuals use certain technologies to create children, and on the living arrangements they will attempt for those children. The present arrangement between courts and legislatures for regulating family formation does not provide certainty as to what a court might determine under the rubric of "best interests." The only assurance now possible is that judges—nonparticipants in the formation of a particular child's family— will decide, unless we and our partners in parenthood agree to resolve our conflicts over our children.

I will propose a theory of legal intervention (or nonintervention) in assisted reproduction that is family-centered and ideologically neutral. My thesis is that the reproductive technology revolution challenges legal institutions to develop new constructs, but that the basic social institution of the family remains intact—as far as law is concerned—even though ethical conflict remains within our society about the uses of reproductive technology. The hard issues—such as whether genetic or gestational parenting is *the* defining characteristic of "mother"—are difficult issues for both legislatures and courts, which, to protect the family in its many varieties, should take a minimalist approach to using law to resolve the conflicts arising from the use of assisted reproduction. Furthermore, I will argue that courts have, in fact, arrived at a consensus about how legal conflicts arising from the use of reproductive technology should be resolved, and that legislatures should respect this consensus.

More generally, there is a growing agreement among courts about the family and assisted reproduction. Judges will find a way of assuring some minimal level of parental responsibility (not "rights") when there is a dispute over the custody of a child born of assisted reproduction. Judges will not treat disputes over frozen embryos as if they were matters of "family law." Thus, the courts will allow agreements between adults about their disposition, including their destruction, to be enforced. This policy of enforcement of agreements regarding embryos and lack of enforcement of surrogate parenting agreements is not inconsistent. Rather, it is the implicit recognition by courts of the importance of the family as a social institution and the limited role of law in its formation.

Legislatures considering the drafting of any statutes should use the same type of institutional analysis to ensure that parental responsibility remains, even when "collaborative reproduction" breaks down. Even where legislatures permit some form of surrogate parenting agreements to be enforced, a general theory that families can be formed solely through "intent" has not been adopted.[6] Where legislatures have prohibited surrogate parenting agreements, courts are correct in interpreting these statutes narrowly. They are not seen to cover issues associated with the disposition of embryos. There is no need for a constitutional theory of rights to resolve these ethically troublesome cases. As a matter of fact, I believe that constitutional analysis should take a back seat in order to allow proper legislative and judicial analysis of issues associated with assisted reproduction.

Human cloning is now a technical, although difficult to realize, possibility. Legal theorists have already proposed solutions to future human cloning scenarios,[7] without assessing the frameworks legislatures and judges have used to resolve conflicts arising during the use of existing techniques of assisted reproduction. Legislation, in my opinion, will not be able to prevent someone from trying to clone another human being, and perhaps succeeding. My reasoning does not suggest, however, that courts or legislatures should encourage the use of human cloning for any particularly beneficent purpose, and certainly not for general "scientific advancement." On the contrary, my method of analysis suggests that the subject of assisted reproduction raises fundamental issues about the nature of the institution of the family, an institution which thrives best when law minimizes the amount of interference with its formation. The concept of family, as we know it, will adapt by necessity to encompass the changing nature of family as an institution under law. It is up to us to recognize that fact, and not look to legislatures or courts to declare one or another kind of family formation as "illegal."

THE RHETORICAL CALL FOR LEGISLATIVE SOLUTIONS

Assisted reproduction has fascinated both the media and legal scholars since the case of *Baby M*. As one judge noted, there have been more law review articles written on problems of assisted reproduction than there are actual reported litigated cases.[8] Judges nonetheless insist that legislatures might or should provide more effective solutions for the ethical confusion many of these cases raise.

A recent Massachusetts case, *R. R. v. M. H.* (a case in which the court used pseudonyms to protect the privacy of the minor), in which the court ruled that a surrogate parenting agreement was unenforceable, illustrates the point.[9] As in *Baby M*, the married woman who had signed an agreement to serve as the surrogate through artificial insemination for an infertile couple changed her mind about "giving up" the child to the sperm donor and his wife. The father of the child and his wife filed a lawsuit seeking to have the terms of the surrogate agreement (giving custody to the father) enforced in court. The lower court granted temporary custody to the father and his wife pending the appeal to the higher court on the question of the legality of the surrogate agreement in Massachusetts.

Unlike the *Baby M* agreement, the Massachusetts agreement provided that the surrogate would forfeit her entire $10,000 payment for "her services" if she ever asserted her parental rights in court. There were other "factual" differences between the *Baby M* and the Massachusetts agreements, such as allowing the surrogate to have contact with the child and providing for the $10,000 payment to be made through installments. None of these differences were significant to the highest Massachusetts court, which ruled that the agreement was unenforceable while calling for the legislature to resolve the issue: "A Massachusetts statute concerning surrogacy agreements, pro or con, would provide guidance to judges, lawyers, infertile couples interested in surrogate parenthood, and prospective surrogate mothers."[10]

As the Massachusetts court notes, after the *Baby M* case, a small number of legislatures enacted statutes covering some aspects of surrogate parenting contracts. In its assumption that a "pro or con" position is the main issue before legislatures, the Massachusetts court characterizes the statutes along this continuum of pro or con enforcement of the agreements. Using this framework, one might conclude that eight states (Alabama, Arkansas, Florida, Iowa, Nevada, New Hampshire, Virginia, and West Virginia)[11] have allowed the enforcement of surrogate parenting "agreements" under certain conditions, and the District of Columbia and nine states (Arizona, Indiana, Kentucky, Louisiana, Michigan, Nebraska, North Dakota, New York, and Washington) have prohibited surrogate parenting agreements.[12]

But if we analyze in detail any of these statutes with the view of treating them as a source of policy,[13] they are not as different as the Massachusetts court might suggest. Even those states which the Massachusetts court asserts are "pro" surrogate parenting agreements have narrow provisions. The New Hampshire statute, for instance, requires judicial preapproval of the surrogate parenting agreement,[14] allows the surrogate to change her mind for seventy-two hours after delivery,[15] and limits the amount of payment to her.[16] What little is known about the practice of surrogacy from infertility clinic reports would suggest that without some payment, the practice of surrogacy is not commercially viable.[17] The requirement of judicial preapproval implies that there might be some circumstances in which a judge might disapprove of an agreement. Add the idea that the surrogate can change her mind after birth, and we are far from the notion of "freedom of contract" as the guiding principle of the legislation. None of these statutes could be treated as standing for the proposition that "principles of contract" should govern disputes over children born of assisted reproduction.

On the other hand, New York's barring of surrogate parenting agreements, provides a "weak" notion of legislative prohibition. One way of thinking about the nature of a prohibition is to ask what the consequences are for violating it. The penalties provisions of the New York statute are quite minimal for all of the participants: a $500 fine for the various kinds of mothers and fathers who might be involved,[18] and a $10,000 fine for brokers for a first-time offense.[19] The physicians and their assistants are not sanctioned under the statute at all.[20] As a matter of fact, if there is no payment to the surrogate and no broker, there are no sanctions against anyone.[21]

The results of these legislative enactments are very weak prohibitions in the New York statutory scheme, and highly regulated agreements in the New Hampshire statutory scheme. Both statutes result from some type of compromise between various interest groups. The fact that the practice of surrogate parenting is still alive and well in New York, and that New Hampshire has not become a hotbed of surrogate parenting, comes as no surprise once one understands the nature of statutes surrounding families.

The Massachusetts court notes several types of statutes that might argue for its public policy result of nonenforcement of surrogate parenting agreements, pointing to both statutes governing adoption and artificial insemination.[22] However, the court does not make explicit its theory of judicial and legislative balance in matters regarding the family. I propose that the opinion makes sense if we assume that the question about the degree of legal intervention in assisted reproduction is primarily a matter for legislatures. The public policy choice before the Massachusetts court is whether courts, legislatures, or the "market for assisted reproduction" is the primary forum for public policy resolution. Among the three institutions, the market—social practices, notions about science, medicine, and "choice"—is the primary determinant of social behavior. Among legal institutions, legislatures are better equipped than courts, since the regulation of social practices should ultimately be decided by market or representative democratic processes.

When the legislature has not acted, the Massachusetts court is entitled to delineate the correct "public policy," so long as it does not make its ruling on constitutional terms. The Massachusetts court quite properly framed the issue as one of a custody dispute and decided the legal issues in accordance with the ways in which most custody disputes are resolved.[23] The court had to "make the law," but it was entitled to make only as much law as was required without necessarily changing the custody result. As in *Baby M*, the father in the Massachusetts case was allowed to have primary custody under family law principles, even though he could not use the agreement to prevent the surrogate from asserting her claim to visitation of the child she had borne. In other words, legislation regarding family matters provides guidance to courts on how to resolve issues which private parties themselves have not been able to resolve.

In the end, the Massachusetts court's analysis helps explain the less-than-finite statutory language of the New York statute regarding conflicts over custody: "In disputes between the genetic mother, the birth mother, the genetic father, etc. . . . the court is not to treat the birth mother's signing of a surrogate parenting contract as adverse to her claim.[24] This language fails to instruct the court as to whether the genetic or gestation mother is the "real" mother, but the language fulfills the purposes of the legislative and judicial institutional settlement in matters related to family.

This type of institutional settlement between courts and the political process differs from other areas such as commercial contracts, racial and gender discrimination, termination of pregnancy, or physician assistance in death. Whether a question is primarily for the judiciary, the legislature, or some other institution requires a comparison of the alternatives, rather than a presumption in favor of judicial competence, which the tendency to constitutionalize the issue of assisted reproduction does.

ENFORCING AGREEMENTS ABOUT EMBRYOS

Kass v. Kass,[25] decided after New York enacted its Surrogate Parenting Agreement Act, [26] is the first appellate court decision on the disposition of frozen embryos[27] in which the court had to consider the broad claim of whether there was a policy or principle *against* enforcing agreements in assisted reproduction cases. Prior to agreeing to cryopreserve some of the Kasses' embryos after several other forms of in vitro fertilization had failed to produce a pregnancy, the clinic had the Kasses sign an additional "consent" document. This document provided that the Kasses were to decide jointly what to do with any unused embryos, and added that if the Kasses failed to agree, the clinic would be allowed to use the embryos for research on ways to improve assisted reproductive technologies and presumably afterwards destroy them.

Some of the frozen embryos were implanted in Mrs. Kass's sister, who had agreed to be a "gestational surrogate." When the sister did not become pregnant, she refused to be implanted with the remaining frozen embryos. Shortly after her refusal, the Kasses decided to divorce. Mrs. Kass typed up an agreement for what was termed an "uncontested divorce," including some language about what was to be done with the frozen embryos.[28] Three weeks later, however, Mrs. Kass filed a lawsuit seeking to have the court declare that she had the right to have the frozen embryos implanted in an attempt to achieve a pregnancy.

The trial judge initially ruled that the wife had exclusive jurisdiction over the frozen embryos on two broad grounds. First, the judge interpreted *Davis v. Davis*,[29] a highly celebrated case in Tennessee about the disposition of frozen embryos, as establishing the authority of courts to "balance" the interests of the wife seeking to implant the embryo in herself against the interests of the husband in not becoming a genetic parent. Second, the trial judge reasoned that the wife had some type of constitutional right to control what happened to her body, which included the right to implant the embryos created with her ovum and the sperm of her soon-to-be ex-husband.[30]

New York's highest court summarily overruled the trial judge's constitutional ruling based on the United States Supreme Court's abortion opinions. The New York court considered a new argument proposed by Mrs. Kass's lawyer: that the Surrogate Parenting Contract Law embodies a broad principle against enforcing any agreement regarding embryos. The unanimous New York court ruled that the particular agreement in this case clearly indicated that the frozen embryos should be "donated" to the fertility clinic for use in its research program in the event of a disagreement among the gamete donors. At a more general level, the court informs infertility clinics that agreements about frozen embryos will be enforced, at least, as between the gamete donors, despite a legislative policy in New York declaring surrogate parenting agreements "void and against public policy."

The New York court was justified in treating the dispute between the Kasses as a simple case of contract interpretation for broader theoretical reasons. First, in its description of the "legal landscape generally," the court acknowledged that the disposition of embryos and assisted reproduction are generally matters for legislatures rather than for judges.[31] The court had to resolve the dispute because only judges can grant a divorce. Second, the New York court is engaging in providing guidance to lower courts about how to resolve these issues which may arise in the absence of specific New York statutes. The court rejects the idea put forth by commentators that there are any constitutional issues involved. In so doing, it rejects the analysis of the Tennessee court in *Davis*, a similar postdivorce dispute over embryos, that embryos are entitled to "special respect."[32] The more general proposition that the New York Court of Appeals promulgates is that statutes dealing with assisted reproduction are to be narrowly construed. Assisted reproduction is not an area in which the courts can move any faster than the legislatures in adapting the law to changing social, technological, and economic conditions.

Anticipating that there might be disputes in the future, the New York court laid down two institutional rules: The "ultimate policy" in matters affecting assisted reproduction is for legislatures; and existing statutes on assisted reproduction about surrogate parenting or artificial insemination are to be narrowly construed. In effect, lawyers will fill in the "gap" and must take care to ensure that they understand the framework the courts and legislatures are using in dealing with assisted reproductive technology.

In simple terms, this means that Mrs. Kass cannot use New York courts to help her establish the family she apparently wants (e.g., a relationship with a biologically related child). If Mrs. Kass is to have the biological family she desires, she must find private individuals willing to collaborate with her. From the perspective of law, embryos are not children, although they may embody some adults' deepest hopes and dreams about the future. Agreements about embryos are enforceable because, from a legal perspective, embryos have no families.

STATUTES AS A SOURCE OF POLICY FOR DISPUTES

Successful assisted reproduction does not necessarily lead to a successful marriage, as illustrated by recent cases in Connecticut and California where divorcing couples argued over the custody and economic support of children born through different assisted reproductive technologies. The courts had to resolve both these cases by looking at statutes surrounding issues of the family in order to achieve the sensible result of providing economic support for children and appropriate custody arrangements.

In the Connecticut case, *Doe v. Doe*,[33] seven years after the birth of a child born from a "voluntary" surrogate arrangement, the husband sought a divorce and claimed exclusive custody on the ground that the child was "not a child of the marriage" as required by that state's divorce statutes. By arranging in a separate legal proceeding to have the parental rights of the surrogate mother terminated, the husband took the position that he was the only legal parent of the child that he and his wife had raised for seven years. The wife had maintained primary custody, with visitation for the husband, during the course of this extensive litigation. By the time Connecticut's highest court decided the case, the child was fourteen years old. Not surprisingly, the court looked at various Connecticut statutes on custody to arrive at the result that the wife had some claim to custody, despite her lack of any biological connection to the child.[34] The court presumed that the Connecticut legislature operated under the assumption that the text of its statutes incorporated the basic notion that "family" means "adults caring for children."

In the California case, *Buzzanca v. Buzzanca*,[35] the Buzzancas arranged to have a surrogate gestate an embryo with no genetic connection to them or the surrogate mother. Shortly before the child's birth, the husband filed suit for divorce claiming no financial responsibility for the child who was born shortly thereafter. In the preliminary legal skirmishes before the divorce, the trial judge ruled that the Buzzanca child had no parents.[36] The appellate court called this ruling an "astonishing" result, and reversed the decision. The trial judge's "no parent" result must be explained in terms other than perverseness. I suspect that the trial judge was in search of an "institutional guide" and found uncertainty in the California cases regarding assisted reproduction.

In one of the most celebrated surrogate parenting cases, *Johnson v. Calvert*,[37] the California Supreme Court decided that a gestational mother without any genetic connection to the embryo was not the legal mother. Mrs. Calvert, who had provided the ovum for the embryo, and Mr. Calvert, the sperm donor, were declared the legal mother and father of the child given birth to by Johnson. The media and many commentators hailed the *Johnson* case as standing for the broad proposition that adult agreements about assisted reproduction can create a family. Some went so far as to suggest that surrogate agreements were enforceable in California.[38] Furthermore, another California case involving surrogate arrangements suggested that the lack of any biological connection to the child was fatal to an adult's claim to parental status before the law.[39] It was the inconsistent rhetoric of the prior cases that led the trial judge in *Buzzanca* to his legal conclusion that a child of assisted reproduction could have "no parents."

To overcome this absurd result in the context of a divorce, the *Buzzanca* appellate court had to interpret California case law on assisted reproduction in light of various statutory provisions. In this analysis, *Johnson v. Calvert* involves the question of how "mother" is defined under the Uniform Child Custody Act when two women claim to be the mother.[40] Previous cases involving child support issues of children born through artificial insemination were illustrative of the court's authority to impose economic obligations on a divorcing husband who consented to artificial insemination of his wife. The California legislation on artificial insemination basically affirmed this approach of making the husband who consents to artificial insemination the legal father. The court further noted the absence of any specific legislation governing in vitro fertilization or surrogate parenting in California. As a result, the long opinion concludes that in the absence of legislation directing otherwise, the court is entitled to hold that the husband in a voluntary assisted reproductive arrangement is the father of the child, at least for the purposes of determining child support obligation following divorce.[41]

For those who view assisted reproduction from the perspective that "children of choice" are to be protected through law, *Buzzanca* arguably raises the issue of whether the "family by intent" doctrine applies to an oral contract for surrogate parenting. For those who share the view that the family is too fundamental a social institution to be defined by legal institutions, the *Buzzanca* court faces an issue which had been addressed in previous instances of assisted reproduction: Who pays for children?[42] This question is one of long standing for law, and should not be lost in our fascination with the ability of modern science and medicine to assist or rearrange the biology of reproduction. Biology does not, and should not, rule law when it comes to the institution of the family, even in the constitutional sense.

THE CONSTITUTIONAL CONTEXT:
FATHERHOOD

To illustrate how central a legislative definition of parenthood is, I discuss briefly the case of *In Re Michael H. v. Gerard D.*,[43] in which Michael H., the biological father of a child, tried to challenge the legislative definition of "father." The case began in California. Michael H. did everything possible in his own mind to be a father to his child, Victoria. A few months after Victoria's birth, her mother, Carole—who was then married to Gerard D.—and Michael each had blood tests, as did Victoria. These tests indicated a 98.07 percent probability that Michael's sperm provided the genetic material for Victoria's conception. During the first year of Victoria's life, she lived with Michael and her mother for just two months. The remainder of the time, Victoria lived with her mother in a variety of places. Sometimes Victoria's household included Gerard D., and other times another man. When Victoria was one-and-a-half years old, Michael filed a lawsuit in state court in California to establish his fatherhood and to gain a legal (court-ordered) right to see her on some regular basis. After he filed his lawsuit, Michael, Victoria, and Carole once again lived together, off and on, for almost eight months. Nearly two years after Victoria's birth, Carole and Michael signed a stipulation agreeing that Michael was Victoria's father. One month later, however, Carole ordered her attorney not to file the stipulation with the court, and took Victoria to live with her husband.

The court appointed a guardian ad litem for Victoria. Joining forces with Michael, this lawyer asked that Victoria be allowed to visit with Michael pending the ultimate outcome of the litigation. The court granted limited visitation. As the litigation continued, Carole's husband, Gerard D., became an active participant and intervened as a party to the lawsuit. Gerard claimed that he was Victoria's father—using the definition of fatherhood found in California statutes—and asked the court to dismiss Michael's claim of fatherhood. The state courts agreed with Gerard that the California statute declaring that a child born to a wife living with her husband is legally the child of her husband, and therefore determined that Michael's request to be named as Victoria's legal father should be dismissed, without hearing anything about his relationship to Victoria or considering the significance of the blood tests.

Both Michael and Victoria's court-appointed guardian raised constitutional objections to the operation of the California statute preventing
Michael from acting as one of Victoria's fathers. The United States Supreme Court rejected both claims in *In Re Michael H. v. Gerard D.* In effect,
the Court held that the political process—legislature—is the primary policymaking body for determining the legal father of a child whose mother
is married. The majority of the Court ignored the blood tests which indicated that Michael was most likely the biological progenitor of Victoria.
In legal definitions of fatherhood, legislatures can—without violating the
Constitution—consider the social and economic consequences to children
in general as more significant than the genetic connection to a particular
child.

In defining the Supreme Court's role in the public debate about the
meaning of fatherhood, the three justices writing opinions for the majority posed different questions stemming from their divergent views of
the role of marriage in the lives of children. For purposes here, I will
deal only with the opinion of Justice Scalia because he clearly delineates
the legislative prerogative regarding adult/child relationships. Even
though Justice Scalia's rhetoric has great significance in terms of constitutional theory, we should not ignore the question that underlies the
structure of his opinion: Are sperm donors fathers?

For at least a century, long before the invention of sophisticated blood
tests, the California legislature has been considering the possibility that
questions of paternity might arise. Since 1872, there has been a premise
embedded in California legislation which essentially states that the child
of a married woman who is living with her husband is "presumed" to
be her husband's child.[44] The modern version of this legislation provides
for blood tests to determine who the father is when there is some dispute.
California legislation was different from similar legislation in other
states, in that California courts had interpreted its statutes to mean that
a non-spouse like Michael could not use blood tests to dispute the paternity of a child whose mother's husband was willing to declare the
child his in a court. In other words, Michael was denied the opportunity
to demonstrate to a court that it would be in Victoria's "best interests"
for her to have some contact with him.

This lack of court access to resolve the conflict between Michael, Gerard, and Carole over Victoria's life does not, under Justice Scalia's theory, result in a denial of anyone's constitutional rights. The California
legislation, in Scalia's view, was designed to protect the sanctity of the
family unit, defined as a legal marriage with children. Justice Scalia ac-
cepts the legislative determination that raising children within a marriage is generally good for children. Furthermore, in his view it is
legitimate for the state to use its powers to protect the marital unit from
interference from outsiders, even if the outsider might be the biological

progenitor of one of the children. In effect, a legislature can declare that all of Gerard's and Carole's children stand in the same legal relationship to them, regardless of where their genes came from. By the time the litigation reached the Supreme Court, Justice Scalia points out, Carole and Gerard had two other children and were living in New York. As long as Carole and Gerard, a married couple, were willing to join together in a united front against Michael's claim of fatherhood, Justice Scalia held they were entitled to use the legislative presumption of Gerard's fatherhood against Michael. In sum, Scalia favors a legislative presumption of fatherhood over a biological one.

As abstract propositions, there is little to question in Justice Scalia's reasoning, when we consider that biological and legal fatherhood are quite often the same category. Victoria's court-appointed law guardian sought to assert an independent constitutional right to continue some contact with Michael, or at least an opportunity to demonstrate that he was her biological father, while accepting that Gerard remained her legally-presumed father. Justice Scalia dismissed the law guardian's argument because it implied that the state courts—public bodies—would have to recognize that Victoria might have multiple legal fathers. The constitutional argument fails in Scalia's opinion because: "whatever the merits of the guardian ad litem's belief that such an arrangement can be of great psychological benefit to a child, the claim that the State must recognize multiple fatherhood has no support in the history or traditions of this country."[45] Justice Scalia's opinion is based on institutional, not individual, concerns.

FAMILIES IN COMPLEX DEMOCRACIES

Consider whether a court should allow the female partner of an admitted lesbian to adopt the biological child of her partner, born through the process of anonymous artificial insemination. Adoption—a creation of legislatures—requires courts to look at statutes enacted at various times to determine if the institution of family can mean that a child has "two legal mothers." Should a court interpret the existing statutory provisions on adoption as enacting a policy that permits individual agreement among adults to define a child's family?

In *Matter of Jacob*,[46] the highest court in New York decided a case involving the legality of lesbian adoption. In the same decision, it also decided a case involving the adoption of a female partner's child by an unmarried male. In both cases, the lower courts had interpreted the various statutes as creating an incentive to marry or a disincentive to attempt parenting without marriage. In more technical terms, the courts ruled that neither the male nor female partner met the statutory definitions of individuals who could petition a court to become a parent by adoption. The New York State highest appellate court overruled the lower court rulings.

In doing so, the court interpreted the complex statutory scheme surrounding adoption as creating an "underlying public policy of providing a parent-child relationship for the welfare of the child."[47] In the court's view, the statutory language—"an adult unmarried person or an adult husband and his adult wife together may adopt another person,"—meant a single person or a married couple are eligible to adopt.[48] Or put another way, any adult can file a petition for adoption of a particular child, but a married person *must* be joined by his or her spouse when filing an adoption petition. In so delineating the legislative purpose, it is important to emphasize the narrowest of the legal points: the legislature authorized a judge to consider when it is in a particular child's best interest for a particular adult to be the child's parent.

In both lesbian-and heterosexual-couple adoptions, the social dynamics surrounding the lower courts' rulings were unlike the *Baby M* case because there were no conflicts between the adults seeking to be adoptive parents and any biological parents. In the case of the heterosexual couple, the biological father of the child had consented to the adoption, and her mother had joined the adoption petition.[49] The prospective father had been living with the child and her mother for more than three years at the time of the petition for adoption. In the case of the lesbian couple, one of the women had borne a child through artificial insemination by an anonymous donor. The genetic father is unknown and the biological mother had consented to the adoption. The two women had been sharing the parenting responsibility for nearly three years at the time of the filing of the petition for adoption. The court's opinion marshaled a variety of sources to support its conclusion that any ambiguity in the statutory language should be resolved in favor of the child's having the opportunity to be adopted.[50]

This interpretation of existing legislative schemes regarding the family is, of course, controversial, as the vigorous dissent in *Matter of Jacob* demonstrates.[51] The dissent interprets the very same language quoted above as meaning that the lesbian couple cannot adopt because they cannot legally marry, and the male petitioner for adoption can adopt only after he marries the child's mother. To reach its result, the dissent began from the perspective that heterosexual marriage is the foundation of the institution of the family[52] and interpreted the same statutes differently in the course of the argument.

The dissent, however, assumed that the New York legislature had joined a few states that have a very different policy regarding adoption by homosexuals. Some states, for instance, have enacted statutes prohibiting homosexuals from adopting.[53] New York, on the other hand, has an administrative regulation—not a statute—specifically prohibiting discrimination against prospective adoptive parents on the basis of marital status or sexual orientation.[54] New York also has recent legislation acknowledging "open adoption"—allowing a biological parent to retain visitation rights after adoption.[55]

Certainly, no legislative action should be taken without data, and without the sense that, at times, legislative action is not the best course in the interest of preserving the institution of the family that is child-centered. A complex society demands a similar system of balances. The lack of legislative action often creates equilibrium.

Themes of liberty and tradition form our constitutional legacy. Modern legislatures are rightly cautious before acting. While these admittedly conflicting themes are not directive of a particular policy regarding, say, lesbian adoption, they do at least suggest that a static impression of parenthood cannot be the basis of public policymaking either. Rather, a legislature must gain some realistic understanding of the present state of parenthood, recognizing that its capacity for knowledge is limited simply because legislatures are public, while families, at least in democracies, are private and intimate. The legislature must then consider the present institutional structure of parenthood within law. Here, undoubtedly, the "traditional view" that marriage has some relationship to family structure—and provides economic and legal protection for children—cannot simply be swept away by anecdotal accounts of many successful instances of raising children outside of marriage in alternative lifestyle homes.

Nontraditional adoption demonstrates how easily questions of public policy become defined as debates about "values," or more specifically, "family values." I suggest that we try to refocus on the institutional definition of the problem which requires two different kinds of inquiries: First, we must agree on what the public policy problem is. Such definition poses a set of questions for possible legislative action. Defining the problem around a child-centered definition of family points to a line of questions that makes legislative action more difficult because our institutional arrangements for democracy require respect for both liberty and tradition. From the institutional perspective of the family, a court might answer the question of nontraditional adoption either "yes" or "no," depending upon the circumstances of the individuals involved.

Second, we must consider the institutional costs of changing any given judicial result, be it one allowing adoption by an unmarried person or one disallowing the sharing of legal responsibility for child rearing by two women, two men, or an unmarried man and woman. The problem becomes a question of whether general solutions by legislatures lead to better overall social results than court resolutions of individual petitions for adoption. This question is a difficult one, since the lack of definitive legislative resolution affects the number of petitions for adoption that single persons and their partners will file.

Some physicians, for instance, will provide anonymous semen donations to single women without inquiry, knowledge, or interest in the particular woman's sexual orientation. Some lawyers will advise lesbian women who have used artificial insemination to file or forgo adoption petitions, depending upon those lawyers' interpretation of court rulings on lesbian adoptions in their particular state or jurisdiction. But more important, some individuals will use self-administered artificial insemination without the assistance of physicians and will raise children with whomever they choose, without regard to the partner's legal relationship to their biological children.

CONCLUSION

Creating a child has become either more or less marvelous, depending upon one's perspective. Equally disturbing is the convergence of the public and private in the act of creation, as well as in the consequences. But the resolutions in the *Baby M* case and other surrogacy cases, or the failures of adults to agree about what should happen to frozen embryos, should not signal a need for public policy decision making. We still need to determine what the public policy problem really is.

For legal decisions, I have argued that we should define family by its institutional meaning, which delineates "parental" responsibility for children. This child-centered definition of family allows political or legislative decisions about parenthood to be made with maximum consideration for the intimate connections with those we call family. Such consideration begins to restore the notion of privacy to our intimate lives. More important, this child-centered definition of family as an institution allows legal decision makers to distinguish between the social and legal importance of marriage (a public institution) from the family (a very private institution), although marriage nonetheless is entitled to some protection from state interference.

It is imperative to make these distinctions. A constitutional argument based simply on one's contribution of sperm is difficult in part because law attributes significance to sperm only after the genetic material manifests itself in new life, a child. In determining "parenthood," the New Jersey Supreme Court was correct in rejecting William Stern's argument that he had a constitutional right to have his artificial insemination agreement with Mary Beth Whitehead-Gould enforced in court. As a state court, however, the New Jersey Supreme Court relied on its interpretation of state statutes to arrive at the solution declaring that Baby M had two biological parents—a father with whom she lives and a mother whom she visits periodically. Mr. Stern's marriage to Mrs. Stern remains a public fact; their family relationships are private and inviolate.

Inviting legislative consideration—but not necessarily requiring legislative action—is an appropriate judicial response to a complex public policy issue. It considers all the implications of new ways of conceiving children. Simultaneously, such consideration respects the competing visions of family. A legislative analysis of public policy regarding family creation must hear themes of liberty and traditions while listening to discordant views of interest groups.

Legislative analysis is imperative in an age in which our beginnings are biotechnologically complex: public policy options must be created as well as explored. Generational continuity posits choices throughout life, as well as at its end: prolonging life and physician-assisted death are personal decisions with public policy implications. As I probe these ethical issues, bear in mind that my mode of analysis cannot negate "traditional" values or contemporary scientific realities. Nor can I deny the loss of self that occurs with debilitating conditions or aging. The continuity of life means that I must acknowledge losses as well as gains.

When it comes to the institution of the family, individual decisions to become parents are obviously influenced by economic and social incentives. But these decisions may be equally driven by notions of individual continuity—egos—that are mysterious to others as well as to individuals. *The family as an institution*, however, is currently arranged, and periodically rearranged, through courts and legislatures. In a world of diverse family arrangements, our sense of community will come only if we pay attention to institutional arrangements that are clearly matters of public concern.

NOTES

1. *In the Matter of Baby M*, 109 N.J. 396, 469, 537 A. 2d 1227, 1264 (1988).

2. *Kass v. Kass*, 91 N.Y. 2d 554, 696 N.E. 2d 174, 673 N.Y.S. 2d 350 (1998).

3. *R. R. v. M. H.*, 426 Mass. 501, 689 N.E. 2d 790 (1998).

4. *Buzzanca v. Buzzanca*, 61 Cal. 1410, 72 Cal. Rptr. 280 (1998).

5. *Doe v. Doe*, 246 Conn. 652, 717 A. 2d 706 (1998).

6. Janet L. Dolgin, *Defining the Family: Law, Technology, and Reproduction in an Uneasy Age* (New York: New York University Press, 1997), 176–212.

7. John A. Robertson, "Liberty, Identity, and Human Cloning," *Texas Law Review* 76 (1998): 1371–456.

8. *Kass v. Kass*, 91 N.Y. 2d 544, 563.

9. *R. R. v. M. H.*, 426 Mass. 501, 689 N.E. 2d 790 (1998).

10. Ibid., 513.

11. Alabama: Code of Ala. § 26-lOA-34 (1999); Arkansas: Ark. Stat. Ann .§ 9–10–201 (1997); Florida: Fla. Stat. § 742.15 (1998); Iowa: Iowa Code § 710.11 (1997);

Nevada: Nev. Rev. Stat. Ann. § 126.045 (1998); New Hampshire: N.H. Rev. Stat. Ann. § 168-B:16 (1999); Virginia: Va. Code Ann. § 20–159 (1998), Va. Code Ann. § 20–160 (1998); West Virginia: W. Va. Code § 48–4-16 (1999).

12. District of Columbia: D.C. Code § 16–402 (1998); Arizona: A.R.S. § 25–218 (1998); Indiana: Ind. Code Ann. § 31–20-1-1 (1998), Ind. Code Ann. § 31–20-1-2 (1998); Kentucky: K.R.S. § 199.590 (1998); Louisiana: La. R.S. 9:2713 (1998); Michigan: M.O.L. § 722.855 (1998); Nebraska: R.R.S. Neb. § 25–21, 200 (1998); North Dakota: N.D. Cent. Code § 14–18–05 (1999); New York: N.Y. C.L.S. Dom. Rel. § 122 (1999); Washington: Rev. Wash. Code § 26.26.230 (1999), Rev. Wash. Code § 26.26.240 (1999).

13. Whether statutes should be used as a source of policy guidance in deciding cases is a matter of considerable controversy among legal scholars. To get a flavor of the debate between those who see legislation as a matter of principle and those who adopt a more pragmatic view, compare Ronald Dworkin, *Law's Empire* (Cambridge, MA: Belknap Press, 1986) to William Eskridge and Phillip Frickey, "Statutory Interpretation as Practical Reasoning," *Stanford Law Review* 42 (1990): 321–84.

14. N.H. Rev. Stat. Ann. (1999), 168: B-16 § I(b).

15. N.H. Rev. Stat. Ann. (1999), 168: B-25, § IV.

16. N.H. Rev. Stat. Ann. (1999), 168: B-25, § V.

17. Cynthia B. Cohen, ed., *New Ways of Making Babies: The Case of Egg Donation* (Bloomington, IN: Indiana University Press, 1996), 1–48.

18. N.Y. C.L.S. Dom. Rel. (1999), § 123(2)(a).

19. N.Y. C.L.S. Dom. Rel. (1999), § 123(2)(b).

20. N.Y. C.L.S. Dom. Rel. (1999), § 123(1)(b).

21. N.Y. C.L.S. Dom. Rel. (1999), § 123(1) does not allow a person to "knowingly request, accept, receive, or give any fee, compensation or other renumeration" in connection with arranging a "surrogate parenting contract."

22. *R. R. v. M. H.*, 426 Mass. 501, 510.

23. Note that in the case, the court pointed out how a court can approve a custody agreement, and how it was careful not to disturb the "compromise" on visitation while making its ruling on the legality of the surrogate agreement. *R. R. v. M. H.*, 426 Mass. 501, 505.

24. N.Y. C.L.S. Dom. Rel., § 124.

25. *Kass v. Kass*, 91 N.Y. 2d 554. N,Y. C. L. S. (1999) Dom. Rel..

26. N.Y. C.L.S. Dom. Rel., §§ 121–24.

27. *Davis v. Davis*; 842 S.W. 2d 588 (Tenn. 1992) is the first case of a divorcing couple dispute which raised the issue of "embryo agreements," and has been widely commented on. But Tennessee, unlike New York, did not have any statutory provisions regarding surrogate parenting agreements.

28. *Kass v. Kass*, 91 N.Y. 2d 554, 560.

29. *Davis v. Davis*, 842 S.W. 2d 588 (Tenn. 1992).

30. The trial judge's rulings are described in the intermediate appellate court opinion, *Kass v. Kass*, 235 A.D. 2d 150, 154 (1998).

31. *Kass v. Kass*, 91 N.Y. 2d 554, 562 (1998).

32. Ibid., 563.

33. *Doe v. Doe*, 244 Conn. 403, 717 A. 2d 706 (1998).

34. Ibid. 422–423.

35. *Buzzanca v. Buzzanca*, 61 Cal App. 1410.

36. Ibid., 1410, 1412.

37. *Johnson v. Calvert*, 5 Cal. 4th 84, 851 P. 2d 776, 19 Cal. Rptr. 494 (1993).

38. Richard A. Epstein, "Surrogacy: The Case for Full Contractual Enforcement," *Virginia Law Review* 81 (1995): 2305–41, 2307, n5.

39. *In Re Marriage of Moschetta*, 216 Cal. App. 2d 383, 30 Cal. Rptr. 2d 893 (4th App. Div. 1994).

40. *Buzzanca v. Buzzanca*, 61 Cal. App. 4th 1410, 1421.

41. Ibid., 1424.

42. This was particularly the case in artificial insemination. As the *Buzzanca* court notes, a New York judge ruled that the lesbian partner posing as a man for the purposes of artificial inseminate was responsible for child support. 61 Cal. App. 4th 1410, 1419 citing *Karin T. v. Michael T.*, 127 Misc. 2d 14, 484 N.Y.S. 2d 780 (1985).

43. *Michael H. v. Gerard D.*, 491 U.S. 110 (1989).

44. The statute, then Cal. Evid. Code Ann. § 621(a) (West Supp. 1989) and now Cal. Fam. Code § 7540 (1996), reads, "the issue of a wife cohabitating with her husband, who is not impotent or sterile, is conclusively presumed to be a child of the marriage."

45. *Michael H. v. Gerard D.* 491 U.S. 110, 131.

46. *Matter of Jacob*, 86 N.Y. 2d 651, 660 N. E. 2d 397, 636 N.Y.S. 2d 716 (1995).

47. Ibid., 658 (quoting *Matter of Robert Paul P.*, 63 N.Y. 2d 233, 236 [1984]).

48. N.Y. C.L.S. § 110 (1999).

49. *Matter of Jacob*, 86 N.Y. 2d 651.

50. Ibid., 665.

51. Ibid., 669 (Bellacosa, J., dissenting).

52. For example, Judge Bellacosa said of both couples that "[t]heir relationships lack legal permanency and the State has not endowed them with the benefits and enforceable protections that flow from relationships recognized under color of law. Nowhere do statutes, or any case law previously, recognize de facto, functional or second parent adoptions in joint circumstances as presented here." Ibid., 669. He went on to cite, for "contextual understanding," that New York recognizes neither common law nor same-sex marriage (Ibid., 671), and that "marriages and single parent households are not, after all, mere social conventions generally or with respect to adoption circumstances; they enjoy legal recognition and special protections for empirically proper social reasons and public policies." Ibid., 673.

53. In New Hampshire, for example, "any individual not a minor and not a homosexual may adopt." N.H. Rev. Stat. Ann. § 170-B:4 (1995). Moreover, the New Hampshire Department of Health and Human Services is expressly forbidden by the state legislature from granting a license to any foster home with one or more homosexual adults. Ibid., § 161:2 (IV) (1995). See also Florida Stat. § 63.042 (2)(d)(2)(3) (1995) ("no person eligible to adopt under this statute may adopt if that person is homosexual").

54. N.Y. C.R.R. 18, § 421.16(h)(2) (1995).

55. The Court of Appeals had ruled that New York statutes did not permit

open adoption. *In Re Gregory B.*, 74 N.Y. 2d 77, 91 (1989). A year later, the legislature set up procedures for allowing the surrender of parental rights with the retention of rights of visitation according to agreements between biological and adoptive parents. N.Y. Soc. Serv. § 383-c (2) (1996).

_____ Chapter 3 _____

Creating One's Own Death: Is There a Constitutional Right to Die?

Do Americans have a *constitutional* right to die?
Ronald Dworkin[1]

Much has been written recently on the subject of choice in dying: Who has the right to choose? Under what circumstances does another—physician, guardian, officer of the court—make that choice? And how will your choice affect me or my mother or my children?[2]

Ronald Dworkin, professor of law at New York University and professor of jurisprudence at Oxford University, argues that there should be a constitutional right to die. In *Life's Dominion: An Argument about Abortion, Euthanasia, and Individual Freedom,* he suggests that the Court's opinions on abortion and terminating medical care support his own belief that physicians and competent patients should be able to agree about the timing of the patient's death.[3] He, along with five other "leading philosophers," filed in the United States Supreme Court a brief in the physician-assisted suicide cases arguing that supposedly voluntary agreements would not undermine secular notions of the sacredness of human life necessary for the functioning of our complex democracy. They urged the Court to declare unconstitutional statutes making physicians' assistance in this agreed-upon death a crime.

Despite the fact that the Supreme Court rejected the philosophers' argument, Professor Dworkin maintained afterwards in a *New York Review of Books* essay that the Supreme Court, or at least a majority of the justices, had not rejected his basic contention that the "liberty" expounded in the Court's abortion opinions meant there is something called "a constitutional right to die."[4] I do not intend to argue with Professor Dworkin or anyone else as to whether *Roe v. Wade* was correctly decided. I believe a woman's constitutional right to decide whether to terminate a pregnancy is good public policy, good for the children who are born, and even good for the varieties of families to which we belong.

I will, however, suggest that Professor Dworkin's affirmative answer to his own question is bad public policy. A constitutional right to die—whatever that might mean—cannot change the fundamental distinction between giving birth and dying. Many believe that through their actions and choices, they can create (or to use the modern euphemism, "plan") their children, while some of their neighbors believe each child is a "gift" or "burden" from the ultimate Creator. It is possible—but not without enduring controversy—to suggest that the state's regulatory processes should have a minimal role in deciding which children should be born to whom. Using constitutional law to minimize the roles of regulatory and legislative processes in adults' decisions about whether to become parents seems axiomatic in my view of the role of law in our lives. A constitutional right to an abortion is only a part of this fundamental way in which we think about our togetherness, our larger covenant as a political and social community.

But dying differs from procreative choices and arrangements. I want to trace the legal arguments that have created the fusion of the two in instances of procreation and separately in dying. I will suggest a path towards resolving our subsequent social and ethical quandary—a path that is open to each of us through an institutional approach.

Dworkin's views of the larger compact can be stated in terms of two broad developments. The first part is the status of a woman's choice prior to the Court's pronouncements on terminating medical care in 1990. The second part of the development, evident in the Court's most recent pronouncement on abortion in 1993, puts to rest, at least for the moment, the question of whether the Court will overrule *Roe v. Wade*. Although the legal parameters for a woman's choice about pregnancy and all our choices surrounding death are different, I propose a synthesis that explains how law—constitutional law—can be used to protect the variety of families in which we live and die in our complex community.

Rather than ask Professor Dworkin's question of whether we have a constitutional right to die, I ask if the Court is the proper *locus* for the public debate on living and dying. Such a focus would establish that constitutional law is in the background, not the foreground, of intimate questions of personal meaning individuals ask themselves about birth, infertility, health, illness, dying, death, and even gender. The political—the legislative—process ought to become the focus of public analysis which deals with the larger questions regarding generational continuity in our lives and deaths.

Professor Dworkin has correctly indicated that justices of the United States Supreme Court have different theories of the Constitution, even when they agree about how a case should be decided. He does not, however, entertain the possibility that the justices ask different kinds of questions in constitutional cases that are dependent on the nature of the problem.

Justices O'Connor, Rehnquist, and Scalia all agreed in 1990 that the Missouri scheme for terminating the care of an incompetent patient was constitutional in *Cruzan*.[5] Each justice wrote a separate opinion because each asked different questions about the role of the Court and other legal institutions in the process of dying. A year earlier, in *Webster v. Reproductive Services*,[6] the same three justices agreed that a Missouri statute declaring that life begins at conception was constitutional, but again wrote three different opinions to arrive at the controversial result. In 1993, however, when the Court was faced squarely with the question of overruling *Roe* in *Planned Parenthood of Southeastern Pa. v. Casey*,[7] the trio parted company in terms of the result. Justice O'Connor not only refused to overrule *Roe*, but also held unconstitutional a legislative provision requiring married women to notify their husbands of their intention to abort. Justices Rehnquist and Scalia, for different reasons in their dissenting opinions, would have held that provision constitutional. Focusing on the differences between these supposedly "conservative" justices illuminates how their institutional positions—not their theories of liberty—shaped subsequent constitutional debates about the role of physicians in our lives and in our dying.

THE CHOICE OF DEATH

Nancy Cruzan had the kind of nightmarish death most people fear. After she was admitted to a hospital following a serious car accident, she lingered in a nursing home unable to communicate with anyone before dying after seven years under professional care. Following her hospitalization, while she was in a comatose state, her husband divorced her, and her parents became her legal guardians. Their conflicts with the Missouri state officials who operated the nursing home where Nancy spent most of the last years of her life led to court battles at various levels of the state system, and eventually to the United States Supreme Court.

While her parents lost the legal battle in the Supreme Court, a Missouri trial judge afterwards agreed that they could remove the food and nutrients sustaining Nancy Cruzan in her persistent vegetative state. Nancy was buried at the age of thirty-three. Her institutional life in hospitals and nursing homes—influenced by decisions in various courts and the legislature—illustrates much about the capacity and limitations of the institution of law, particularly constitutional law, in matters of dying and death.[8]

Cruzan's parents (or more accurately, their lawyer), argued in the United States Supreme Court that Nancy Cruzan had a constitutional right to die. They constructed this argument from the Court's prior decisions on abortion, state court cases on terminating care, and scholarly articles relevant to the topic.[9] The Court did not simply refuse to accept the Cruzans' argument; the five-person majority did not believe that the parents were even asking the right question. To understand the majority opinion in *Cruzan*, I have followed the advice of the great German poet, Rilke, and learned to live their questions. Among the majority, there were three questions which emphasized different facets of the case.

When Should Courts Terminate Treatment?

For the author of the majority opinion, Chief Justice Rehnquist, the question depended first upon an assertion that Nancy Cruzan, in her persistent vegetative state, was not a competent person, but rather an incompetent patient:

The difficulty with petitioners' claims [those of Nancy Cruzan's parents] is that in a sense it begs the question: An incompetent person is not able to make an informed and voluntary choice to exercise a hypothetical right to refuse treatment or any other right.[10]

The Court in effect swept aside all prior cases about the "rights" of competent patients relied upon by the Cruzans' lawyers and asserted that Nancy Cruzan's inability to speak meant someone else had to speak for her.

Even though Nancy was legally an adult, her parents—as her legally appointed guardians—could make most, but not all, of her decisions. Rehnquist does not, however, consider the question in the case as one of the Court choosing the next best decision maker for silent patients. Rather, his framing of the question involved not simply a deference to the judgments of the state legislatures and courts about how certain types of patient decisions should be made, but also a belief that these legal entities are better equipped than the United States Supreme Court to determine how decisions for silent patients should be made. Justice Rehnquist's deference to the political process in one particular state rep-

resents an assessment that it is the least detrimental alternative for deciding about when a patient should die.

The fact that the Missouri legislature had passed a Living Will Statute
which purported to deal with the issue of when patients could terminate
treatment was significant for Chief Justice Rehnquist. Within this piece
of legislation was a provision about how a specific form of medical treatment—food and hydration—should be terminated for incompetent
patients like Nancy. This provision weighed heavily in Chief Justice
Rehnquist's view of all the circumstances. The Missouri political process,
while producing a number of legal procedures for terminating care, provided that before food and hydration could be terminated for an incompetent patient, a court must find by clear and convincing evidence that
such termination was in accordance with the silent patient's wishes.

Rehnquist affirmed the Missouri Supreme Court's finding that Nancy's
statement regarding not wanting to live if sick or injured made to her
roommates several years before her accident was insufficient evidence to
meet this judicial standard of proof. For Justice Rehnquist, the risk of
keeping some silent patients alive who might have wanted to die is not
as bad as the risk of conscious human efforts to bring about the death
of those patients who might have wanted to live, even in a persistent
vegetative state.[11]

The political process gave state judges the function of sifting through
past statements and actions to determine the patient's intentions regarding the termination of food and hydration. For Justice Rehnquist, the
question became whether this delegation to judges of the ultimate power
is unconstitutional. Given that question, it comes as no surprise that
Rehnquist can speak in glowing terms of Nancy's parents, and yet hold:
"[A] State may apply a clear and convincing evidence standard in proceedings where a guardian seeks to discontinue nutrition and hydration
of a person diagnosed to be in a persistent vegetative state."[12] Nothing
in his opinion precluded the Missouri courts from determining in a subsequent hearing that Nancy's parents had met the evidentiary standards
six months after the Supreme Court opinion, when they presented new
witnesses to the trial judge. And nothing in his opinion precluded other
justices who agreed with his conclusion about the constitutionality of the
Missouri scheme as applied to Nancy's case from seeing other questions
in this institutional drama.

When Should a Person Other than the Patient
Terminate Treatment?

Justice O'Connor's concurring opinion raises a distinct question because she makes a different assertion in *Cruzan* than her colleague, Chief
Justice Rehnquist. Justice O'Connor asserts that medically injected food

and water—she chooses the term "artificial provision of nutrition and hydration"—is the same as any other kind of medical treatment.[13] She focuses on the bodily intrusion required to insert a feeding tube. In the case of a competent and verbal patient's expressed objections, this would clearly be a violation of Justice O'Connor's notions of constitutional liberty.

But the question she asked was: Under what circumstances does the Constitution require a state court to accept a surrogate decision maker's representation of the patient's constitutional right to decline treatment? In her view, the Missouri rule requiring clear and convincing evidence was a constitutional means of exercising the comatose patient's will. She wrote separately to emphasize that other states' rules, particularly those that allow a surrogate decision maker to order hospitals and physicians to remove food and nutrition without a high level of judicial scrutiny, were also constitutional.[14] Moreover, Justice O'Connor's opinion is a clear invitation to the political process to consider alternative means of protecting the incompetent patient's right to refuse treatment in light of the Court's holding that one state's practice is constitutional.

Her question, as compared to Chief Justice Rehnquist's, places a different emphasis on the institutional status of the constitutional rights of patients, both competent and incompetent, to refuse treatment. Her analysis of liberty warns legislators and state court judges to take the claims of incompetent patients seriously, even though in this case, she is unwilling to declare unconstitutional a state system which places a strong burden of proof on the surrogate decision maker. While individual states' processes are clearly preferable to a constitutional adjudication of these issues, she, unlike her colleague, Justice Scalia, leaves the door ajar for a constitutional challenge.

Should Treatment Ever Be Terminated?

Justices Rehnquist and O'Connor deliberately framed the question in *Cruzan* in a manner rendering discussion of the Court's many opinions on abortions unnecessary to their conclusions. On the other hand, Justice Scalia constructed the question in the case to ensure that his view of the Court's institutional failure in abortion would be explicated and condemned. He defined the issue not only in terms of science's increased capacity to keep the human body alive, but also in terms of the Court's previous declarations about the legislative response to abortion:

From the tenor of today's opinions, we are poised to confuse that enterprise as successfully as we have confused the enterprise of legislating concerning abortion—requiring it to be conducted against a background of federal constitutional imperatives that are unknown because they are being newly crafted from Term to Term.[15]

As a consequence of this concern, he characterizes any decision to end treatment, even when death is a relative certainty, as a self-inflicted killing—a suicide.[16] In his view, political and regulatory processes can take steps to prevent a person from taking his or her life. For him, the constitutional constraints on that political process are minimal. The question presented in *Cruzan* for Scalia is whether the methods used by Missouri to prevent her—or her parents—from ending her life are unconstitutional. There is no deprivation of her "liberty without due process" because "there is no significant support for the claim that a right to suicide is so rooted in our tradition that it may be deemed 'fundamental' or 'implicit' in the concept of ordered liberty."[17] Justice Scalia's response is an attempt to defeat the position raised in the dissenting opinions, one of which indicated that the Court's opinions on abortion stood for a larger constitutional principle protecting the doctor-patient relationship.[18]

A CHOICE FOR WOMEN ONLY

A year before the Court issued its opinion in *Cruzan*, the media had convinced many people that the Court would overrule its famous decision on abortion, *Roe v. Wade*.[19] In 1989, scholars and journalists predicted enormous changes in our lives resulting from the forthcoming constitutional pronouncements of a supposedly more "conservative" Supreme Court. Very little attention has been devoted since then to delineating the questions our constitutional decision makers—the justices themselves—were asking prior to *Cruzan*.

In *Webster v. Reproductive Services*[20] the same trio of justices—Rehnquist, O'Connor, and Scalia—wrote opinions upholding the constitutionality of a legislative declaration that "life begins at conception." Justices Rehnquist and O'Connor construed this legislative provision—part of a recently-enacted Missouri statute on abortion—as irrelevant to a woman's constitutionally declared right to have an abortion.[21] At the same time, but for very different reasons, both justices found constitutional principles to uphold the constitutionality of a legislative provision instructing physicians to test for viability at twenty weeks of gestation before performing an abortion. Both Rehnquist and O'Connor reached their conclusions without overruling the decision in *Roe*. Justice Scalia, on the other hand, was the only justice joining the five-vote majority judgment in *Webster* who wanted to use the case to overrule *Roe*. Prior to *Cruzan*, the evolving constitutional principles of abortion had at least three themes, built around three questions asked by this trio of justices:

Can Legislatures Prefer Childbirth over Abortion?

Justice Rehnquist's opinion for the Court in *Webster* leaves a bipolar legacy. On the one hand, it is a highly technical decision about when constitutional issues are ripe for adjudication by the Supreme Court. It reduces, for instance, important public concerns about abortion to whether a certain clause in one provision of a 1986 version of a Missouri statute on unborn children and abortion is constitutional.[22] On the other hand, *Webster* provides a method of understanding the different questions people ask about abortion, and which public means are legitimate for solving these differences. Many of those questions cannot—and I will argue should not—be resolved by one constitutional pronouncement.

Justice Rehnquist framed the many questions in *Webster* from the perspective that the case represented the fourth time a Missouri statute on abortion had been before the United States Supreme Court.[23] The "life begins at conception" language, found in the preamble of a 1986 act on unborn children and abortion, was thus viewed as part of the continuing dialogue between the Court and state legislatures about the scope of the legislative authority in the post-*Roe* world.[24]

The question for Justice Rehnquist became: Do any of the Court's many decisions interpreting *Roe* prohibit state legislatures from expressing a public policy that favors childbirth over abortion? Since the Court had previously held that *Roe* did not require states to provide Medicaid payments for abortion on the basis of a policy preference for childbirth, Justice Rehnquist's declaration that the preamble of the Missouri statute did not infringe upon a woman's constitutional right to abortion was supported by the Court's precedents.[25]

But as to *Roe* itself, Justice Rehnquist provided a qualification and a new interpretation when he ruled that a provision requiring physicians to determine viability of a twenty-week-or-more-old fetus before performing an abortion was constitutional.[26] Justice Rehnquist rejected an interpretation of *Roe* in which the authority of legislatures to regulate abortion was dependent upon the trimester of pregnancy in which the abortion was performed.[27] By asking the question of whether the Constitution allows a legislature to prefer childbirth over abortion in the post-*Roe* world, Justice Rehnquist can uphold a statute that defines viability at twenty weeks as opposed to *Roe*'s statement that viability be at twenty-three weeks, without overruling the basic holding of *Roe* that the political process cannot make performing an abortion a crime under all circumstances. In so doing, Rehnquist proclaimed that future attempts to use *Roe* would be analyzed from the perspective of a not yet fully articulated theory of "liberty."

This constitutional liberty analysis implies great deference to legislative or political decisions, not for abstract philosophical reasons, but as a means of delineating the Court's institutional role in public policy-making surrounding the issue of abortion. A liberty analysis of abortion, however, is subject to various interpretations, as Justice Scalia's concurring opinion in *Webster* demonstrates.

Who Is Sovereign on Terminating a Pregnancy?

Justice Scalia takes to task his other four colleagues in the majority in *Webster* for failing to overrule *Roe*. His view that *Roe* was a wrongheaded interpretation of the Constitution feeds the popular conception that "conservative" justices are simply waiting for another opportunity to overrule *Roe*. The world Scalia envisions once *Roe* is overruled might be, from Justice Rehnquist's perspective in 1989 (an original dissenter in *Roe*),[28] an institutional disaster for the Court. But those institutional concerns—delineating the Court's role in public policymaking about abortion—are not central to the question Justice Scalia is considering. He is not simply asking a "technical" question of whether a case—*Roe*—should be overruled, but a larger question about authority for decision making. If one asks why Justice Scalia not only believes *Roe* should be overruled, but also answers so vehemently in the affirmative, one sees that he is asking a question about sovereignty: Which power structure should control abortion?[29]

While sarcastically referring to Justice Rehnquist's outcome as "a triumph of judicial statesmanship," Justice Scalia writes:

It is not that, unless, it is statesmanlike needlessly to prolong this Court's self-awarded sovereignty over a field where it has little proper business since the answers to most of the cruel questions posed are political and not juridical—a sovereignty which therefore quite properly, but to great damage to the Court, makes it the object of the sort of organized public pressure that political institutions in a democracy ought to receive.[30]

When compared to Justice Rehnquist, Justice Scalia has a rather mechanistic view of the public policymaking process. Justice Rehnquist's approach sees *Roe* as having set up a dynamic relationship between courts and legislatures over the issue of abortion. Recall that *Roe* was decided over Rehnquist's dissent in 1973. In 1989, he was trying to work with the existing institutional dynamics on a case-by-case basis, hoping to evolve towards new constitutional principles. Justice Scalia, by contrast, is focused only on the institution of courts, particularly his Court, and seeks to restore the Court to its proper place of public respect by removing it altogether from the political mess in which it is embroiled. As for abortion, Scalia votes for an institutional exit, whereas Justice Rehnquist votes for a more limited role for judicial review. Justice Scalia saves his most biting critique for Justice O'Connor's concurring opinion. Her views of constitutional law indicate that he cannot rely upon her to join his deconstruction of "the mansion of constitutionalized abortion law, constructed overnight in *Roe v. Wade*."[31]

Can Legislatures Prohibit the Use of Contraceptive or Reproductive Technologies?

Justice O'Connor's opinion in *Webster* starts with the assumption that women and men have a constitutional right to decide about childbearing. Her notion of liberty treats constitutional law as a shield against certain political decisions about when life begins. Unlike her four dissenting colleagues in *Webster*, she did not see the Missouri statute as a violation of those constitutional rights. In her view, the dissenters' fears that Missouri's preamble to its abortion and unborn children statute could be used in violation of constitutional pronouncements on the use of contraceptives was unfounded.[32] She went on to say: "Neither is there any indication of the possibility that the preamble might be applied to prohibit the performance of in vitro fertilization."[33]

Note that O'Connor framed the question in terms of whether this particular piece of legislation interfered with previous Court decisions, some of which preceded *Roe*, about the unconstitutionality of legislative restrictions on contraception. Unlike Rehnquist, she did not see the decision to uphold the provision on viability as being in conflict with prior decisions, although she admitted that *Roe*'s "trimester" solution to the abortion issue was "problematic."[34] Her concurrence is a critique of the way in which Justice Rehnquist uses the court's previous decisions to uphold Missouri's latest legislative enactment over abortion. Justice O'Connor's question in *Webster*, however, indicates that there is at least a third way of looking at the abortion controversy that recognizes the complexities of modern life.

MOTHERHOOD

In *Planned Parenthood of Southeastern Pa. v. Casey*,[35] Justice O'Connor, writing an opinion for the Court, upheld—by the narrowest of margins—all the provisions of a recently enacted Pennsylvania abortion statute except for one: the provision requiring a married woman to notify her husband of her intention to have an abortion. Justices Rehnquist and Scalia wrote separate dissenting opinions, because each believed the section of the law requiring wives to notify their husbands about an impending abortion *was* constitutional. Under the divergent theories of Justices O'Connor, Scalia, and Rehnquist, the following legislative provisions became constitutional: (a) requiring facilities that perform abortions to provide certain data to regulatory authorities; (b) requiring a twenty-four-hour waiting period prior to an abortion; (c) requiring parental consent for a minor who seeks an abortion; and (d) requiring physicians to provide information about fetal development prior to obtaining a woman's consent to an abortion. Only husband notification—not spousal veto power—divides Justice O'Connor from Justices Scalia and Rehnquist.

Justice O'Connor's view in *Casey*, that motherhood and spousal relations are distinct within the institution of law, was adhered to by four other justices of the Court. Rejection of the theories of Justices Rehnquist and Scalia by a majority of the Court illustrates more clearly that Justice O'Connor's opinion—the current prevailing view of the United States Supreme Court—is about the constitutional significance of the biological differences between men and women, particularly about the protection of motherhood from political domination. In so doing, the Court established itself as the primary policymaking forum for abortion issues without rejecting totally the role of political processes in the abortion debate.

Can Legislatures Give Husbands a Legal Interest in Conception?

Justice Rehnquist's entire theory, as noted in the *Webster* decision, gives a great deal of deference to political decision making, while acknowledging that a woman has a constitutional "liberty" interest in terminating a pregnancy. The issue of whether a legislature can constitutionally require a wife to *notify* her spouse is simply a matter of whether one can say it is "irrational" for the legislature to do so. Having concluded it is constitutional—i.e., rational—for the political process, for instance, to require that the woman be told about fetal development prior to having an abortion, he asks simply whether it is rational to require wives to inform husbands of their intentions to terminate a pregnancy. Chief Justice Rehnquist suggests that the political process can construct rules based on the assumption that most wives do, in fact, inform their husbands of intended abortions. But his framing of this particular problem in the abortion controversy—husband notification, not husband veto power—was rejected by the majority of the justices of the Court.

Is Liberty a Tradition?

It should come as no surprise that Justice Scalia vehemently—and with rhetorical flourish—asserts in *Casey* that *Roe* should have been overruled as he had also proclaimed in *Webster*.[36] Nor is his opinion in *Casey* particularly newsworthy in its scathing attack on Justice O'Connor and her colleagues for holding the spousal notification provision unconstitutional.[37] What is significant in his *Casey* dissent is his assertion of a general theory of constitutional liberty that protects, in his institutional view, the Court from the political process and any public policy role in abortion.

It is perhaps best to dissect the soul of his theory by hearing Justice Scalia's own voice:

[T]he issue in this case: is not whether the power of a woman to abort her unborn child is a 'liberty' in the absolute sense; or even whether it is a liberty of great importance to many women. Of course, it is both. The issue is whether it is a liberty protected by the Constitution of the United States. I am sure it is not. I reach that conclusion not because of anything so exalted as my views concerning the 'concept of existence, of meaning, of the universe, and of the mystery of human life.' [citation to majority opinion omitted] Rather, I reach it for the same reason I reach the conclusion that bigamy is not constitutionally protected—because of two simple facts: (1) the Constitution says absolutely nothing about it, and (2) longstanding traditions of American society have permitted it to be legally proscribed.[38]

As to the legislative provision requiring wives to notify husbands, Justice Scalia informs his colleagues and other interested parties that the Court can only ask if it is rational for legislatures—political bodies—to believe that marriage is protected if wives inform husbands of their intentions regarding childbirth. Long standing tradition allows for legislatures to regulate the marriage relationship. In Scalia's view, a woman's abstract claim to a liberty interest must fall to tradition.

Is Motherhood a Distinct Legal Category?

Consider the issue Justice O'Connor addresses before declaring only one provision of the Pennsylvania abortion statute unconstitutional: As to children that a husband and wife might raise together, both are equal for the purposes of constitutional law.[39] But when the issue is whether political bodies have the authority to order that husbands have some potential decision-making role, she states: "Before birth, however, the issue takes on a very different cast. It is an inescapable biological fact that state regulation with respect to the child a woman is carrying will have a far greater impact on the mother's liberty than on the father's."[40] Such a view allows O'Connor to accept the judicial fact findings of lower courts about the possible adverse impact of this spousal notification provision. The implication of her opinion is to reject the traditional view of the woman's role in family life as a part of her husband, or of marriage as a single entity headed by the husband.[41] As she states, "Women do not lose their constitutionally protected interest when they marry."[42] For all adult women, the decision to become a mother is to some degree constitutionally protected.

With all the changing views of marriage and relationships taking place in the larger society, Justice O'Connor is unwilling to remove from constitutional scrutiny decisions of a current political majority about family and marriage. Her opinion in *Casey* in fact asserts a constitutional right to terminate pregnancy simply because men and women have a different biological relationship to childbirth in a world in which the social and economic status of women is in transition. In blunt terms, judicial constraints on political decisions about women's decisions to terminate a pregnancy are a function of the fact that women gestate children while men are sperm donors. As a result, these inviolable biological facts must be taken into consideration as politicians weigh the conflicting demands of various groups and individuals when legislating on abortion. The current theory of constitutional law allows a woman to ask a court to review and correct political decisions about abortion that "unduly burden" her decision to terminate or continue a pregnancy.

CONCLUSION

Do Americans have a constitutional right to die? Professor Dworkin's question has led us into the labyrinthian maze of Supreme Court opinions, many of which—assenting or dissenting—will become points in persuasive arguments for positive or negative answers to the central question. The abortion debate teaches an important lesson about the centrality of law to our most intimate decisions regarding life and death, as seen in *Cruzan* as well as in *Casey*. Whether Justice O'Connor's, or any other, constitutional theory of why women can terminate pregnancy is applicable to terminating medical care of patients is a question that requires a great deal more exegesis. It is clear from *Cruzan* that the Constitution protects the choice of death by those competent to exercise their choice by declining treatment or ordering medical professionals to remove medical interventions. But as to whether *Cruzan* requires that physicians be authorized to assist patients who ask for professional help in killing themselves, I argue for an analysis that goes beyond notions of "constitutional rights."

Our larger covenant as a community grants to a woman who becomes pregnant the authority to decide whether she can be a (good) mother to the human entity growing within her body. The Court has become the primary public policy forum for the abortion debate. As I will demonstrate, the Court has declined the invitation of Professor Dworkin and others to become the primary *locus* for debate on physician-assisted suicide.

NOTES

1. Ronald Dworkin, *Life's Dominion: An Argument about Abortion, Euthanasia, and Individual Freedom* (New York: Vintage Books, 1994), 181.

2. In 1989, I argued that

Legislatures must examine whether special legislation is needed to deal with the criminal liability of physicians and other health care professionals. The reformulation of the standards for criminal liability is a way of establishing the social function of medicine . . . [when we] . . . move to an institutional approach, we can highlight issues that are clearly germane. . . . The challenge is to develop a structure that encourages caring. . . . We need to focus on the capacity for caring, rather than on 'preserving life' or 'death with dignity,' as the ultimate test of the social fabric.

Larry I. Palmer, *Law, Medicine, and Social Justice* (Louisville, KY: Westminister/ John Knox Press, 1989), 107.

3. Dworkin, *Life's Dominion*.

4. Ronald Dworkin, "Assisted Suicide: The Philosophers' Brief," *The New York Review of Books* 44 (1997):41–47.

5. *Cruzan v. Director, Missouri Department of Health*, 497 U.S. 261 (1990).

6. *Webster v. Reproductive Services*, 492 U.S. 490 (1989).

7. *Planned Parenthood of Southeastern Pa. v. Casey*, 505 U.S. 833 (1992).

8. Nancy Cruzan died of "shock, due to dehydration, due to severe head injury" at 3:00 A.M. on December 26, 1990. Robert Steinbrook, "Comatose Woman Dies 12 Days After Life Support Is Halted," *Los Angeles Times*, December 27, 1990.

9. The Cruzans cited *Rochin v. California*, 342 U.S. 165 (1952), for their first proposition, that the Due Process Clause of the fourteenth Amendment to the U.S. Constitution protects individuals against bodily intrusions by the state. Incompetent persons, they continued, retain this protection even though they are unable to express their wishes (citing *Youngberg v. Romeo*, 457 U.S. 307 [1982], and family members are the best surrogate decision makers for them (citing *Parham v. J. R.*, 442 U.S. 584 [1979]). The consensus of state courts outside of Missouri, the Cruzans argued, supported their case on Nancy's behalf, citing *In Re Quinlan*, 70 N.J. 10, 355 A. 2d 647 (1976); *Brophy v. New England Sinai Hospital*, 398 Mass. 417, 497 N.E. 2d 626 (1986); *In Re Drabick*, 200 Cal. App. 3d 185, 245 Cal. Rptr. 840 (1988); *Delio v. Westchester County Medical Center*, 129 A.D. 2d 1, 516 N.Y.S. 2d 677 (1987); and several other state court decisions. See generally Brief for Petitioners, *Cruzan v. Director, Missouri Department of Health*, 497 U.S. 261 (1990) (no. 88–1503).

10. *Cruzan v. Director, Missouri Department of Health*, 497 U.S. 261, 280 (1990).

11. Ibid., 283.

12. "We believe that Missouri may permissibly place an increased risk of an erroneous decision on those seeking to terminate an incompetent individual's life-sustaining treatment. An erroneous decision not to terminate results in a maintenance of the status-quo; the possibility of subsequent developments such as advancements in medical science, the discovery of new evidence regarding the patient's intent, changes in the law, or simply the unexpected death of the patient despite the administration of life-sustaining treatment at least create the

potential that a wrong decision will eventually be corrected or its impact mitigated. An erroneous decision to withdraw life-sustaining treatment, however, is not susceptible of correction." Ibid.

13. Ibid., 288.

14. "At least 13 States and the District of Columbia have durable power of attorney statutes expressly authorizing the appointment of proxies for making health care decisions." Ibid., 290, n. 2. "Thirteen States have living will statutes authorizing the appointment of health care proxies." Ibid., 291, n. 4.

15. Ibid., 292–293.

16. He argues that the refusal to take "appropriate measures necessary to preserve one's life" is a form of suicide. Ibid., 293. One might argue with him that only a lawyer, a person accustomed to constructing events into preexisting categories, would describe a conscious decision to not use a feeding tube as suicide. I will not make this argument, since my point is to demonstrate that his way of valuing human life allows him to delegate to the political process a degree of control over our lives and deaths that I believe is inappropriate in a democratic society.

17. Ibid., 295 (quoting *Palko v. Connecticut*, 302 U.S. 319, 325 [1937]).

18. Ibid., 439.

19. *Roe v. Wade*, 410 U.S. 113 (1973).

20. *Webster v. Reproductive Services*, 492 U.S. 490 (1989).

21. Ibid., 507.

22. Justice Rehnquist and the plurality questioned the logic of recognizing the state's interest in human life only after viability, and thus declared that interest as "compelling" throughout the pregnancy. Ibid., 519. Justice O'Connor disagreed and adhered to a framework allowing state regulation "when viability is possible," Ibid., 528; but Justice Scalia criticized this as irrational and unprecedented: "[s]ince 'viability' means the mere possibility (not the certainty) of survivability outside the womb, possible viability must mean the possibility of a possibility of survivability outside the womb." Ibid., 536 fn.*. Justice Blackmun believed that a state's interest in "those who will be citizens" can realistically be recognized only progressively with the organism's developing ability to think, feel, and survive. Ibid., 552–53. Justice Stevens argued that the "life begins at conception" language in the statute violated the First Amendment's mandate of separation of church and state. Ibid., 566–72.

23. He notes early on in his opinion that in 1973 the Court declared Missouri's statute criminalizing all abortions except those aimed at saving the life of the mother unconstitutional. *Danforth v. Rogers*, 414 U.S. 1035 (1973). Later, in a case to become more important, *Planned Parenthood of Central Missouri v. Danforth*, 428 U.S. 52 (1976), the Court struck down a Missouri law forbidding abortion without the consent of a spouse for a married woman and a parent for a woman under eighteen years of age.

24. *Webster v. Reproductive Services*, 492 U.S. 490, 504 (1989). The second clause of the preamble indicated that the act was to be interpreted so as to avoid conflicts with constitutional interpretations by the United States Supreme Court over a woman's right to obtain an abortion.

25. In *Maher v. Roe*, 432 U.S. 464 (1977), the Court ruled that a State may permissibly use Medicaid funding to reimburse costs of childbirth and "medi-

cally necessary" first-trimester abortions, even when it does not also pay for elective or "nontherapeutic" abortions. "[*Roe*] implies no limitation on the authority of a State to make a value judgment favoring childbirth over abortion, and to implement that judgment by the allocation of public funds." Ibid., 474. (The Court later expanded this holding to excuse a state from funding even *medically necessary* abortions from which Congress had withheld federal funding. *Harris v. McRae*, 448 U.S. 297 [1980].) Citing *Maher*, the Court in *Webster* read the "life begins at conception" language in the preamble to be such a value judgment, not actually purporting to regulate abortion. 492 U.S. at 507.

26. *Webster v. Reproductive Services*, 492 U.S. 490, 513. To uphold this provision, Rehnquist had to suggest that some of the Court's previous opinions interpreting *Roe* were wrongly decided.

27. Although there was not a five-person majority endorsing this particular theory, his reaffirmation of *Roe* deserves repeating in his own words:

The experience of the Court in applying *Roe v. Wade* in later cases . . . suggests to us that there is wisdom in not necessarily attempting to elaborate the abstract differences between a "fundamental right" to abortion as the Court described it in *Akron* [a previous case] . . . , a "limited fundamental constitutional right," which Justice Blackmun [the author of *Roe*] today treats *Roe* as having established, . . . or a liberty interest protected by the Due Process Clause, which we believe it to be. The Missouri testing requirement here is reasonably designed to ensure that abortions are not performed where the fetus is viable—an end which all concede is legitimate—and that is sufficient to sustain its constitutionality.

Webster v. Reproductive Services, 492 U.S. 490, 520.

28. *Roe v. Wade*, 410 U.S. 113, 171 (1972) (Rehnquist, J., dissenting).

29. This is a very powerful statement, which I am taking from Walter B. Wriston's *The Twilight of Sovereignty: How the Information Revolution Is Transforming Our World* (New York: Scribner, 1992).

30. *Webster v. Reproductive Services*, 492 U.S. 490, 532.

31. Ibid., 537.

32. Ibid., 522–23.

33. Ibid., 523.

34. Ibid., 529.

35. *Planned Parenthood of Southeastern Pa. v. Casey*, 505 U.S. 833 (1992).

36. "*Roe* was plainly wrong—even on the Court's methodology of 'reasoned judgment,' and even more so (of course) if the proper criteria of text and tradition are applied." 505 U.S. at 983 (Scalia, J., concurring in part and dissenting in part). He later added, "by continuing the imposition of a rigid national rule instead of allowing for regional differences, the Court merely prolongs and intensifies the anguish." 505 U.S. at 1002.

37. Ibid., 988–89.

38. Ibid., 980.

39. Ibid., 895–96.

40. Ibid., 896.

41. Ibid., 895–98.

42. Ibid., 898.

Chapter 4

Chronically Ill or Terminal? A Question for Legislatures

We are all terminal cases.

John W. Irving[1]

Dr. Jack Kevorkian's conviction of murder will not destroy the implications of his vision for medicine and law. Kevorkian's actions and rhetoric propose that a distinction between those patients who are chronically ill and those whose death is apparently imminent should be irrelevant to law. All "patients," in his view, expect a cure from medicine. When such a cure is not currently available, an individual physician should be the driver who quickly escorts those patients desiring death in the face of medical failure to their "resting place." In Kevorkian's opinion, the ethical or legal right of the physician to assist a patient's death depends solely upon what the individual patient and her physician decides.

At this writing, Kevorkian has responded to the calls of more than 130 chronic sufferers or terminally ill patients. Whether Janet Currens, his thirty-fifth "client" with chronic fatigue syndrome, for instance, had a "terminal illness" as defined by the current state of medical knowledge is, in Kevorkian's view, irrelevant. His role, as he defines it, is to end suffering. Kevorkian has enough institutional resources in terms of media presence and lay following to continue his crusade through others for a new form of professional ethics grounded in the study of death. Chronic sufferers, those for whom modern medicine provides no "cure," are the special beneficiaries of his scientific vision.

The world according to Kevorkian is one in which the death penalty, abortion, and physician-assisted suicide are linked in a scientific understanding of the nature of death. A person with advanced incurable cancer, for instance, might offer to let a medical researcher "test" a new drug for toxicity.[2] Rather than die from a lethal dose of drugs, a death row inmate could choose to donate his body for experimentation or his organs for transplantation.[3] Any restrictions on experimentation on fetuses or embryos should be relaxed so that the promise of "genetic engineering" could be realized: "to preprogram every human conceptus for a long life of guaranteed biological integrity."[4] This understanding of death would point inevitably to the proposition that life, from the moment of inception to the moment of death, can be lived without suffering.

But most important, until the expected benefits of unleashed biomedical research are available, those with chronic conditions should have the benefits of his civil disobedience in the name of a new medical speciality: that which uses its scientific training for "mercy killings."[5] The goal of the Kevorkian movement is not to enact specific legislation, but to create a new institutional arrangement between law and medicine in which the physician-patient relationship is shielded from any form of public regulation.

KEVORKIAN AS INSTITUTIONAL PLAYER

Kevorkian has achieved a certain institutional status, at least in Michigan. By allowing CBS's *60 Minutes* to televise a videotape of him injecting a lethal drug into a person with amyotrophic lateral sclerosis (Lou Gehrig's disease) in November 1998, Kevorkian forced the newly-elected prosecutor to charge him with crimes for the fifth time. The present prosecutor had unseated his predecessor in 1996 by claiming that the prosecutor's relentless pursuit of Kevorkian in the name of "enforcing the law" was a waste of resources, at least until the United States Supreme Court decided the question of physician-assisted suicide.[6]

A recent enactment of a new statute making assisting suicide a crime gave the present prosecutor a more secure legal basis for obtaining a conviction. Kevorkian's de facto legal immunity up until this point, at least in Michigan, is a part of his vision for medicine and a better world where a "planned death" is part of our concept of the "good life." This vision will not die, even if Kevorkian's appeal of his conviction for murder fails and he starves himself to death rather than die in prison, as he has promised to do. Kevorkian's professional career has been shaped by the notion that he is called to play a unique role in the history of medicine's relationship to law. He believes that his three acquittals of charges of assisting suicide are only an indication that "the people" have understood the logic of science's notion of progress which the Michigan legislature refuses to acknowledge: We shall overcome death when physicians eliminate individual suffering.

The Legislature Defers to the Commission

A trial judge, relying on a 1920 Michigan case,[7] dismissed the very first charge of murder against Kevorkian in connection with Janet Adkins's death—his first "client" in 1990—on the grounds that the act of providing the suicide machine was not murder but assisted suicide, and no such crime existed in Michigan. Late in December 1992, after he had assisted more than a half-dozen individuals in dying, the Michigan legislature decided to "cure" what they now saw as an apparent defect in its criminal law: the lack of a specific provision prohibiting assisted suicide.

By the end of February 1993, the governor had signed a bill making the provision of the physical means to help a person take his or her life "criminal assistance to suicide."[8] Another portion of the bill established the Michigan Commission on Death and Dying. Its purpose was to study the ethical and public health questions raised by "voluntary self-termination of human life."[9] The criminal provision and the commission were linked by a provision repealing the criminal prohibition six months after the date the commission made its recommendations to the legislature.[10]

It is not clear why the legislature established the crime of assisted suicide prior to receiving the advice of its commission. Undoubtedly, the media attention to Dr. Kevorkian's and his lawyer's actions created a political crisis. On the one hand, by 1992 it was apparent to everyone that Michigan was one of the few states that did not make assisting suicide a crime. On the other hand, "the right to die" movement had gained some momentum of its own, independent of Dr. Kevorkian. Derek Humphry's *Final Exit*[11] had become a national best-seller, and respectable physicians, such as Dr. Thomas Quill, had publicly acknowledged aiding at least one patient to die by prescribing the barbiturates that Humphry and the Hemlock Society instructed the public to hoard. Enacting a temporary crime of assisted suicide and establishing a study commission gave opponents of assisted suicide a crime with which Kevorkian could be prosecuted. It also gave proponents a second chance to obtain legalization of assisted suicide.

The Michigan legislators designed the commission to be "representative"—at least of the most vocal special interest groups.[12] They charged the commission to consider the "proper aims" of any legislation regarding "voluntary self-termination"[13] and whether to differentiate between withdrawing or withholding treatment and administering medication as a means of bringing about a patient's death.[14] The legislators in effect asked the commission to address the very questions they themselves had been unable to answer in deciding whether to establish a permanent crime of assisted suicide.

Not surprisingly, the final report of the commission in 1994 indicates the commissioners were divided on the main issue.[15] Nine of the twenty commissioners present voted in favor of a report recommending "decriminalization" of "aid-in-dying." Seven voted against the proposed model statute, four abstained, and two members were listed as not present.[16] Nine of the same twenty commissioners voted against a recommendation encouraging the legislature to make the temporary ban on assisted suicide permanent, five voted in favor of the recommendation, and six abstained.[17]

One group of commissioners—nine in number, but not the same group recommending legalization of assisted suicide—provided the legislature with a "procedural safeguards" report that "neither endorses nor opposes assisted suicide: It simply outlines a procedure which could be enacted should the legislature move to decriminalize some form of self-termination in Michigan."[18] These procedures included a narrow definition of self-termination that excluded "active euthanasia"; a process of consultation with a variety of professionals; an oversight role for courts; and a public reporting requirement that included "demographic data about who is choosing self-termination." But again, five commissioners opposed this attempt to avoid resolving the hard substantive question of the appropriateness of legalization of physician-assisted suicide, and six abstained.

Despite the lack of consensus on legalization, the commissioners reached an agreement on an issue related to current medical practice: that the legislature should do something to increase patient and physician access to methods of controlling pain and other "distressing" symptoms of illness. The commissioners suggested that there was a "right" to the treatment and alleviation of pain that was being ignored because health care professionals were not trained in these modern methods. They were explicit in their recommendation that the legal restrictions on prescribing drugs for those with terminal illnesses should be modified.[19] The commission also reached a consensus that the legislature, having confronted the institutional significance of Kevorkian's practice, should establish some policy on assisted suicide. The Michigan legislature failed to enact any such legislative policy until 1998.[20]

Lest anyone label the Michigan legislature as a group lacking in political courage to decide the question, recall that "commissioning ethics" has been a feature of our national love/hate affair with modern medicine and science for more than twenty years. Either from memories of the deaths they have experienced or heard about, most people acknowledge that dying is hard in a personal sense, but it is also hard and confusing when legal institutions try to make order out of this personal turmoil or peace. When the Michigan legislature initially confronted the question of determining the circumstances, if any, under which a physician or anyone else should be legally authorized to respond to a person's request to time his or her death, it chose not to decide. The response of the Michigan courts to Kevorkian may explain this collective "we don't know" from the legislators.

The Courts Grant Prosecutors Discretion

By the time the legislature had enacted its temporary ban on assisted suicide in 1993, prosecutors had indicted Kevorkian with murder or assisted suicide in connection with a number of deaths. Both the prosecutors and Kevorkian had appealed various rulings of trial judges to the highest court in Michigan. In these appeals, the Michigan courts confronted different questions from those faced by the legislature: Are prosecutors authorized to charge Kevorkian with a crime, and if so, what crime?

In February 1992, the prosecutors charged Kevorkian with two counts of murder in connection with the deaths of two middle-aged women who died in October 1991. Sherry Miller, a 43-year-old woman with multiple sclerosis, died by ingesting carbon monoxide. Marjorie Wantz, a 58-year-old woman with a painful pelvic disease, died from a lethal administration of barbiturates through the suicide machine. The deaths took place prior to the enactment of the crime of assisted suicide in February 1993, so these cases were covered by the status of the law in Michigan in October 1991. The trial judge refused Kevorkian's request to dismiss the charges of murder. Kevorkian appealed this ruling to the highest appeals court in Michigan.

The gist of Kevorkian's argument in the appeals court involved a proposed distinction in the legal definition of murder in Michigan. Kevorkian argued that when Marjorie Wantz pulled the string on the suicide machine and Sherry Miller used a screwdriver to release carbon monoxide into her masked face in a cabin in a state park, he did *not* have a "present intention to kill" as required to hold a person guilty of murder.[21] His lawyer further argued that a more recent court ruling cast doubt on the continued validity of the 1920 ruling that a husband who provided his wife/patient with poison to terminate her life had committed the crime of murder.[22] Michigan's highest court accepted the thrust of Kevorkian's arguments that the 1920 ruling was invalid, but relied upon an equally technical analysis to give prosecutors a means of charging Kevorkian with a crime in connection with his "planned deaths."[23]

Under the court's "reinterpretation of the common law," murder would now be distinguished from assisted suicide in Michigan. Persons who provide the means for others to kill themselves should be charged with assisted suicide rather than murder. Those who cause the death of another person through their own actions could be charged with murder. The crime of assisted suicide would have a maximum penalty of five years in prison[24] whereas the crime of murder has a maximum penalty of life imprisonment.[25] Instead of charging Kevorkian with murder, the prosecutor could now consider charging him with the newly announced common-law crime of assisting suicide.

In the same opinion, the court also ruled that the legislatively enacted ban on assisted suicide was constitutional. Kevorkian had already been acquitted in a case brought under legislative ban prior to the expiration of the ban.[26] The practical effect of this ruling was to allow the local prosecutor to continue the third case against Kevorkian under the statute. The jury acquitted in that case, in March 1996.[27] As a result of the appellate decision in the Wantz and Miller cases, the trial judge changed the charge from murder to assisted suicide. Kevorkian was subsequently acquitted of these charges in May 1996.[28]

Michigan's highest court's authorization of the common law crime of assisted suicide is best understood in the institutional context in which it rendered its decision. The court was aware that the Commission on Death and Dying had issued its final report and that the report was inconclusive, making further legislative action unlikely. Authorizing a common-law crime of assisted suicide effectively placed the decision-making authority regarding Kevorkian in the hands of the Michigan prosecutor.

PHYSICIAN AS GANDHI

When Kevorkian testified in his first trial of assisted suicide in connection with the death of 30-year-old Thomas Hyde, he explained: "I follow the dictates of the Nuremberg Code. When your conscience says that law is immoral you don't follow the law. That's what Gandhi said too. And Gandhi got what I'm getting."[29] This moral metaphor invited the jurors to consider Kevorkian's actions as heroic and perhaps prophetic of a new social order in which the individual, with a physician's help, was in control of suffering.

Geoffrey Feiger, Kevorkian's former lawyer, used technology to bring Thomas Hyde's twisted 30-year-old body back to life by showing the jurors a videotape of Hyde—with the help of his live-in companion—in which he expressed to Kevorkian his desire to die, to "end his suffering." Hyde's companion, Kevorkian's sister, and Kevorkian's "assistant" (who videotaped Hyde's consent) all praised Kevorkian as a compassionate and selfless physician, willing to help deliver Hyde from his obvious suffering. In addition, several medical experts even testified in Kevorkian's defense. These witnesses asserted that giving carbon monoxide to relieve the unrelenting pain Hyde had been suffering from Lou Gehrig's disease fit within an exemption from criminal liability in the assisted suicide statute. The Michigan statute in force at the time lists as an "exception" to its prohibitions any act of "prescribing, dispensing, or administering medications or procedures if the intent is to relieve pain or discomfort and not to cause death, even if the medication or procedure may hasten or increase the risk of death."[30] These arguments were forwarded despite the fact that Kevorkian was not a licensed physician in 1993 when Hyde died. Feiger used a combination of legal maneuverings and moral appeals about the centrality of medicine in our lives to prepare the jurors for Kevorkian's essential claim of exemption from the statute's application.

In Kevorkian's view, the physician is essentially a scientist who applies his scientific reasoning and knowledge in the service of individual clients. Dr. Kevorkian began his legal crusade as a young resident in pathology in 1958, when his first proposal was that death row inmates should be given the option of choosing between death on the gallows and death in the scientific laboratory. Death under anesthesia, while physicians and scientists removed organs or conducted experiments, was, in Kevorkian's view, "a more humane way" of dying than the then-prevailing methods of execution—hanging, the electric chair, firing squad, and the gas chamber. Since Michigan was then and still remains a state that does not allow the death penalty, Kevorkian's desire to be a social reformer required him to seek a national audience for his ideas. Kevorkian recently affirmed his commitment to his earlier vision, by lending public support to the efforts of a death row inmate to stay his execution while the courts considered his request to use his body for human transplantation.[31]

While Kevorkian claims to be "neutral" on whether legislatures should authorize death as a punishment for crime, he remains committed to reaping some "social gain" from capital punishment. He suggested, for instance, in his book, *Prescription Medicide: The Goodness of Planned Death*, that understanding "the criminal mind" requires "the study of *all* parts of the intact *living* brain."[32] He has spent considerable time interviewing death row inmates, and even lobbying in California and elsewhere for legislation to allow them the choice between the conventional methods of execution and his vision of medicine's painless death.[33]

THE SUICIDE CLINIC

Kevorkian's choice-for-prisoners ministry met with a great deal of resistance from his professional colleagues.[34] Unabashed, he continued his crusade for capital punishment reform in the 1980s once the imposition of the death penalty resumed in this country. By the late 1980s, he saw the"right to die" movement as fertile ground for expansion of his movement. Just as a prisoner condemned to death should have a choice about the manner of death, a patient condemned to death by the present failure of medicine to provide a cure for her illness should have a choice for a "painless" and socially beneficial death.

Kevorkian has described how his interest in euthanasia preceded his interest in capital punishment reform. Fresh out of medical school, during his year of internship where he had to care for patients rather than analyze their tissues and organs, he encountered a woman dying of cancer:

Euthanasia wasn't of much interest to me until my internship year, when I saw firsthand how cancer can ravage the human body. The patient was a helplessly immobile woman of middle age, her entire body jaundiced to an intense yellow-brown, skin stretched paper-thin over a fluid-filled abdomen swollen to four or five times normal size. The rest of her was an emaciated skeleton: sagging, discolored skin covered her bones like a cheap, wrinkled frock.[35]

This encounter did not inspire him to want to pursue a career in oncology—caring for those with cancer—or medical research into the causes of the physical degradation he had witnessed. He writes instead of another intellectual and professional commitment:

It seems as though she was pleading for help and death at the same time. Out of sheer empathy alone I could have helped her die with satisfaction. From that moment on, I was sure that doctor-assisted euthanasia and suicide are and always were ethical, no matter what anyone says or thinks.[36]

Kevorkian saw, for instance in fetal research, prospective support for organizing a center for research on the fringes of current law and morality. This research, along with his proposed experiments on those requesting euthanasia, should be done in "suicide centers" where licensed medical professionals could legally perform "medicide."

When he learned in the late 1980s of the open practice of euthanasia by physicians in the Netherlands, he conceived the idea of expanding his death row ministry to "include experimentation on willing patients who opt for euthanasia."[37] A 1987 visit to the Netherlands proved somewhat disappointing to the idealistic physician-reformer until he discovered that the Netherlands' guidelines for administering euthanasia included not just the terminally ill, but patients with chronic illnesses such as multiple sclerosis, arthritis, or even bronchitis. Kevorkian returned to Michigan "inspired" by his visit to risk criminal prosecution by assisting terminal patients to commit suicide.[38]

But media interest in Kevorkian was growing. He began to receive requests for help from patients and for interviews from radio and television talk shows around the country. Kevorkian responded to the call from a Detroit woman with multiple sclerosis because he believed that assisting suicide was legal in Michigan, but not in most other states. By late December 1989, the consultation with this unnamed woman afflicted with severe multiple sclerosis had led to videotaped interviews for a national television show of her wish to use Kevorkian's machine to end her life. But according to Kevorkian, members of her family prevented her from actually appearing before television cameras to announce her readiness to use the machine. Nevertheless, the January 1990 nationally televised broadcast of some of the videotapes of their consultations had launched Kevorkian's grass roots movement to recruit clients through media publicity.

The call from Janet Adkins's husband in November 1989 came after an article about Kevorkian's efforts appeared in a national publication.[39] The fact that Alzheimer's made her mentally "terminal" was enough for Kevorkian to accept this 54-year-old Oregonian as his first actual client. The legalization of these acts—providing the suicide machine or the carbon monoxide and mask—is the "all-important first step" towards the establishment of a professional specialty which helps patients meet death. After legalization of professionally-assisted death, Kevorkian would come full circle, giving "birth to the clinic"; an "obitorium" where our deaths become part of medical progress and perhaps a future world without death.[40]

Kevorkian is fond of creating new words to describe what he does in his law and medicine crusade. At yet another appearance before the National Press Club, he proposed that "patholysis," meaning the "elimination of suffering," is the medical service he believes the suicide center will provide.[41] Kevorkian's creation of new words asks listeners to envision a new world. People are asked to have faith that they, or at least their children and their grandchildren, will live better and longer if death row inmates join with other death-parlor donors to allow physicians/ scientists to engage in biomedical research without any restraints. In other words, Kevorkian encourages people to believe that medicine can deliver the good community if only they can overcome their queasiness about using human beings in a utilitarian calculus that posits progress in science as in fact *social* progress. The question that Kevorkian has raised is: Does the concept of community in our diverse society require law to end the suffering of chronic illness by authorizing professionals to kill the sufferers?[42]

THE UNITED STATES SUPREME COURT GRANTS
DISCRETION TO THE LEGISLATURE

After the United States Supreme Court declared that state legislatures—not the Court—had the authority to determine whether any form of physician-assisted death should be legal, Kevorkian continued his provocative challenges to legal authorities. The Court's "no constitutional right to assisted suicide" declaration and increased media attention to Kevorkian's stepped-up efforts to assist dying has led to a new response from political institutions in Michigan.

Despite polls in 1996 indicating that nearly 70 percent of Michigan voters supported legalization of assisted suicide, by fall 1998 that support had dropped to less than 40 percent. As a result, in November 1998 the voters defeated by a three-to-one margin a measure to make Michigan the second state, in addition to Oregon, to allow physician-assisted death. Prior to that popular vote on the initiative, the Michigan legislature had enacted a new criminal assisted-suicide law that became effective in September 1998. This new statute incorporates the institutional history that Kevorkian has created by eliminating some of the "defenses" in the prior statute and allowing prosecutors alternative approaches to Kevorkian or any others who make visible their death-assisting practices.

For instance, the recently enacted statute specifically allows for the prosecution of assisted suicide under the judge-made common-law crime of "assisted suicide," as explained earlier, and for prosecution under the new statutory language.[43] The effect of this provision allows a jury to decide which of two legal theories can be used to convict Kevorkian, depending upon how the facts are developed at trial. In addition, this statutory provision decreases the chances that Kevorkian could make the highly technical arguments on appeal about distinction between crimes that he made in *People v. Kevorkian* in 1996.

The new statute also restricts the kinds of evidence that Kevorkian was able to present in a new trial. Under prior statutes, experts were allowed to testify that administering carbon monoxide might be thought of as "pain relief" because the prior law had allowed for an exception for medication designed to alleviate pain. The new law had no such exception; instead, the new statute provides an exception only for the withdrawal or withholding of medical treatment.[44] As a result, the fact that Kevorkian is not a licensed physician should preclude his being able to present evidence of his own "interpretation" of his acts of injecting a person with a lethal chemical.

These specific changes in the legislation altered the institutional context in which Kevorkian's fifth trial took place. Although initially charged with both murder and assisting suicide, the prosecutor eventually chose only the murder charge. This tactic led the judge to greatly restrict the kinds of evidence Kevorkian was allowed to present in a trial where he represented himself. A guilty verdict was a more possible outcome, but by no means assured. Kevorkian is not simply one defrocked physician challenging the medical establishment and law; he wears the mantle of science and its implicit promise to eliminate human suffering through application of its technologies. Jurors, like most people, fear that modern medicine has forgotten that our termination appears to be in the hands of physicians, particularly as greater longevity increases the possibility of chronic conditions for everyone. These statutory changes, along with an apparent shift in public attitudes, led a jury to convict Kevorkian of murder in March 1999.

CONCLUSION

Kevorkian's many encounters with the legal system reveal how much the model of acute illness dominates our thinking about public policy and the role of law in medicine. Medicine's function is to "cure" either through drugs, surgery, organ transplantation or transfer to hospice for "comfort care" in dying. The many chronic sufferers, especially as life expectancy increases, who need physician assistance in managing their lives, raise a special challenge to the image of the autonomous physician who cannot "control" whether the patient takes prescribed medication or follows dietary restrictions. It also raises the question of how to recognize the signs of distress which require physician rather than patient intervention.

It is now becoming clear even to the media what was apparent in Kevorkian's earliest obscure writings. Kevorkian does not, however, seek the legalization of certain physician-patient agreements to end the patient's life, but rather the restructuring of the relationship of law and medicine. He further seeks the establishment of suicide clinics to allow painless deaths to become social benefits. Having lived long or short lives by eating the fruits of medical research, he proposes people should give back to science their own bodies when their time is near by a signed or videotaped agreement with their physician.

NOTES

1. John Irving, *The World According to Garp* (New York: The Modern Library, 1998), 688.
2. Jack Kevorkian, *Prescription Medicide: The Goodness of Planned Death* (Buffalo, NY: Prometheus Books, 1991), 254.

3. Ibid., 133. See also "National Press Club Luncheon with Dr. Jack Kevorkian and Attorney Geoffrey Fieger," *Federal News Service* (July 29, 1996): Major Leader Special Transcript ("They don't even . . . want to take organs from condemned criminals who want to donate when they're executed. You've got a bunch of insane people running our institutions.").

4. Kevorkian, *Prescription Medicide*, 241.

5. Ibid., 202–203.

6. Challenger David Gorcyca was quoted a week before the election as saying, "Dick [Thompson] has participated in his own political suicide in his attempt to convict Kevorkian." Brian Harmon, "Challenger Belittles Thompson Tough-On-Crime Stance," *Detroit News*, July 30, 1996. Gorcyca defeated Thompson by a massive twelve-point margin in the August 6, 1996 election, which Thompson subsequently admitted was due to the Kevorkian issue. Brian Harmon, "Thompson Pins Loss on Kevorkian Case," *Detroit News*, August 8, 1996.

7. *People v. Roberts*, 211 Mich. 187, 178 N.W. 690 (1920).

8. The bill was codified at Mich. Stat. Ann. prec. § 28.547 (127).

9. Ibid., § 28.547(121), § 1(1).

10. Ibid., § 28.547(127), § 7(5).

11. Derek Humphry, *Final Exit: The Practicalities of Self-Deliverance and Assisted Suicide* (Eugene, OR: Hemlock Society, 1990).

12. The legislature authorized a variety of interest groups—from the Association of Retired Persons (AARP); ACLU; Hemlock of Michigan; Right to Life of Michigan; prosecutor groups; medical societies of nurses, physicians, psychiatrists, and osteopaths; as well as many others—to nominate individuals to serve on the commission. Mich. Stat. Ann., § 28.547(123), § 3(1).

13. Ibid., § 28.547(124), § 4(1)(b).

14. Ibid., § 28.547(124), § 4(1)(b)(iii)(C).

15. The legislators, of course, were not so naive as to actually expect a consensus from this group with such diverse organizational viewpoints. *Final Report of the Michigan Commission on Death & Dying* (Lansing, MI: The Commission, 1994), Preface [unnumbered].

16. Ibid., Part III: Additional Reports of the Commission [unnumbered].

17. The "majority" view remains somewhat elusive since some of the commissioners were instructed by their organizations to represent the organizations' views. Some of these organizations refused to take public positions because their memberships were so divided on the issue. On the other hand, the commission held public hearings throughout the state, and invited experts to address the commission in its attempts to become better informed about the issue. Its own education, however, did not create the kind of group process that would provide the legislature with "expert" advice that pointed in one clear direction. Ibid., Part I: History of the Commission [unnumbered].

18. Ibid., Part III: Report Offering Procedural Safeguards [unnumbered].

19. Ibid., Part II: Points of Consensus [unnumbered].

20. Mich. Stat. Ann. § 28.561a (1998).

21. *People v. Campbell*, 124 Mich. App. 333, 339, 335 N.W. 2d 27 (1983). In this case, a defendant who sold a gun to another person who later shot himself with it was not guilty of murder because the defendant lacked the present intention to kill.

22. *People v. Roberts*, 211 Mich. 187, 178 N.W. 690 (1920). Technically, this case could be read to mean that the husband's furnishing the poison to his wife at her request to end her suffering from multiple sclerosis constituted "murder by poisoning," since that form of murder along with lying in wait, and "felony murder" were classified as first-degree murder. The husband plead guilty to murder, so the question before the court was simply the degree of murder. But since Michigan was one of the few states without the death penalty, the consequence of the judge's decision was simply how long the husband would spend in prison, not whether he would be put to death.

23. The court "overruled" the 1920 ruling that a husband who provided his multiple sclerosis-stricken wife with poison to kill herself—at her request—was guilty of murder. *People v. Kevorkian*, 447 Mich. 436, 494, 527 N.W. 2d 714 (1996) *cert denied* 514 U.S. 1083 (1995). But the court also ruled that the crime of assisted suicide was part of the Michigan common law—that portion of the law of crimes that was to be developed by the courts—since the legislature had specifically allowed courts this power. Ibid., 495.

24. A "common-law" crime is a crime originally defined by judges in England and the United States prior to the practice of codifying these definitions in statutes in the nineteenth century. For instance, "murder" was defined by judges and those definitions codified and later modified by legislatures. According to the Michigan court, any common-law crime for which the legislature had affixed no explicit punishment was punishable by up to five years in prison and $10,000 fine. Ibid., 495.

25. Both first-and second-degree murder are punishable by life imprisonment in Michigan. See Mich. Stat. Ann. § 28.549(317).

26. Kevorkian was arrested in August 1993 for assisting the suicide of Thomas Hyde. He was acquitted nine months later.

27. These prosecutions were for Kevorkian's roles in the deaths of Merian Frederick and Dr. Ali Khalili. The jury returned a "not guilty" verdict on March 8, 1996.

28. Kevorkian was acquitted on May 14, 1996 of the charges stemming from his assistance with the suicides of Marjorie Wantz and Jack E. Miller.

29. Jack Kevorkian, trial testimony, *Court TV*, April 22, 1994.

30. See Mich. Stat. Ann. § 28.547(127), § 7(b)(3).

31. See Mark Curriden, "Inmate's Last Wish Is to Donate Kidney," *American Bar Association Journal* 82 (June, 1996): 26. See also *Lonchar v. Thomas*, 517 U.S. 314 (1996), in which the U.S. Supreme Court upheld his stay of execution.

32. Kevorkian, *Prescription Medicide*, 34. With the resumption of the imposition of the death penalty by the mid–1980s, the predominant method of execution in the United States has become lethal injection, bringing medicine directly into the administration of capital punishment. More than thirty states currently employ this method, including ten which give the condemned prisoner a choice between lethal injection and some other method. There has been no death penalty in Michigan since 1846. See Mich. Const., Art. IV, § 46.

Kevorkian views this move away from electrocution, hanging, gas chambers, and firing squads as only minimal progress. The quality of these executions could be improved if legislators allowed the most qualified individuals—licensed medical physicians—to perform the injections. Kevorkian regards the legislative prohibitions against licensed physician participation as "irrational."

33. See generally Kevorkian, *Prescription Medicide*. He has contacted legislators and governors in more than twenty states. Ibid., 177.

34. According to Kevorkian, he was forced to resign from his residency program at the University of Michigan Hospital and ignored by the "prestigious journals" when he submitted his ideas for publication. Ibid., 38–42.

35. Ibid., 188.

36. Ibid.

37. Ibid., 189.

38. The Dutch physicians were not enthusiastic about his proposed use of euthanasia patients for experimentation. Ibid., 192.

39. See Ned Zimmerman, "Pushing the Button," *Newsweek* (November 13, 1989): 8.

40. Kevorkian, *Prescription Medicide*, 203.

41. "National Press Club Luncheon with Dr. Jack Kevorkian."

42. William F. May, *The Physician's Covenant: Images of the Healer in Medical Ethics* (Philadelphia, PA: The Westminster Press, 1983), 83–86.

43. Mich. Stat. Ann. § 28.561a, § 329a(3).

44. Mich. Stat. Ann. § 28.561a, § 329a(2).

PART II

THE ROLE OF PHYSICIANS IN GENERATIONAL CONTINUITY

Chapter 5

The Role of Physicians in Our Dying: Relievers of "Suffering"?

Why should a spouse or a child or a dedicated health professional be subjected to the threat of a legal proceeding for easing the suffering of a desperately ill person who consciously and rationally asks that the anguish be ended?

Dr. Timothy Quill[1]

Physicians other than Dr. Kevorkian have introduced the term "physician-assisted suicide" and "planned death" into our lexicon. Dr. Timothy Quill, a former director of a hospice care program and a primary care physician, published an article in the highly respected *New England Journal of Medicine* in 1991 detailing his prescribing of barbiturates for a patient with leukemia.[2] Media and public response to this article made Quill a well-respected spokesperson for the "ethics of relieving suffering." In his opinion, law's traditional concerns about how death occurs, expressed in criminal laws prohibiting assisting anyone's death, are archaic. This view eventually led Quill to become the lead plaintiff in *Vacco v. Quill*, the unsuccessful attempt to have New York's statute prohibiting assisting suicide declared unconstitutional.[3]

The physician-led reform movement has a particular view of self-killing: When appropriately regulated, and aided by a licensed physician, suicide is a medical blessing. Self-inflicted death thus loses its questionable moral status if a physician has certified that both the individual's condition cannot be cured or alleviated by modern medicine and that he or she is making a "rational" choice. At these physician-supervised deaths, observers will be able to celebrate the person's death simultaneously with its occurrence.

The Quill saga is an example of how physicians have shifted the definition of their role in dying from "preserving life at all costs" to "relieving suffering." My analysis of the notion of medical suicide that Quill and his fellow physician-reformers would like legislatures to adopt demonstrates that physicians'—rather than individual patients'—definitions of death would be the ultimate guide to public policy and law. Although Quill approaches the interaction of law and medicine from the perspective of a compassionate clinician rather than as Kevorkian's research-scientist, they essentially agree that law must accommodate the needs of physicians to assist patients' deaths.

THE DOCTOR AS FRIEND

Dr. Quill's patient, whom he called Diane in his article and subsequent book, had a form of acute leukemia. The recommended "treatment" for her condition was the following sequence of medical interventions: several courses of chemotherapy, whole-body radiation, and bone marrow transplantation. Dr. Quill reports that when he offered this treatment as a chance of preventing her death, Diane said, "No."[4]

Her rejection surprised Dr. Quill. Unlike some physicians in the 1970s and 1980s, Dr. Quill did not assume he had some legal authority to impose the treatment in his attempt to preserve her life that a court might affirm. Litigation and legislation surrounding the so-called "right to die" over the previous two decades had clearly established patients' legal right to refuse treatment, even when their refusal meant their deaths.[5] Within these legal constraints, physicians' authority was a function of their ability to use rational discourse with patients to arrive at a course of action—or perhaps inaction.

Dr. Quill tried this approach with Diane. As he described the phases of treatment for her form of leukemia, he explained that her chance of surviving this three-pronged ordeal was 25 percent. She still refused. Dr. Quill, as he later explained in his book, thought at the time that a 25 percent chance of life was "better than 'nothing' (i.e., death) and a lot better than the odds of many other treatments we ordinarily do."[6] His training as a physician—he is board certified in internal medicine—in the late 1970s[7] had taught him something about the emotional effects of some adverse news on patients. Dr. Quill speculated that Diane perhaps did not realize that delaying treatment would decrease her chance of recovery to below 25 percent. Perhaps a chance to discuss her rejection of treatment with members of her family might change her perspective on accepting death. She agreed to come back for another consultation in two days.

When Diane returned for her office visit, her husband and only child— a college student—accompanied her. She explained that she and her family had talked extensively about her options and the risks of death. Her response to Dr. Quill's presentation of her medical options was still "no." As the dialogue continued, Dr. Quill surmised that she was "convinced" she would die during one or more of the three stages of treatment. He offered to do what he could to minimize the side effects of the various phases of treatment and to help her be as comfortable as possible. He did *not*, however, tell Diane and her family members that the last four patients undergoing the treatment at the hospital in which he practiced had died during its course.[8] Dr. Quill does not explain why this information about his hospital or the relative success rates of various other centers with this form of proposed treatment was not deemed relevant to Diane or her family members.

Dr. Quill remained disturbed about Diane's forgoing the 25 percent chance of living as a "cancer survivor" because of his professional knowledge about her—her medical history. Over the previous eight years, Dr. Quill had treated her difficulties with depression and alcoholism. This professional assistance had apparently helped her to remain sober for three and a half years. Diane had survived both vaginal cancer as a young woman, as well as growing up in an "alcoholic family." Dr. Quill had seen his patient "fight" to overcome her own alcoholism and depression. He had fully expected her to use those inner resources to join him and his oncologist colleagues in the "fight" to overcome her cancer. After all, as he noted, prior to his diagnosis of her leukemia, his patient "was really living fully for the first time."[9]

Eventually, Dr. Quill began to see the 25 percent chance of survival from Diane's perspective and referred her to a home hospice care program. Having served as the medical director of such a program, he had good reason to believe she would receive appropriate comfort care—pain medicine, blood transfusions, etc.—when and if she needed them. Along with medical assistance during her dying, he also knew her husband and adult son would receive professional support from her caregivers, if and when they requested such help. The referral to hospice care—rather than trying to convince Diane her decision to forego treatment was "irrational"—might have been a fitting end to Dr. Quill's unease about his professional obligations to Diane. The referral had insurance implications, but Dr. Quill remained her "attending physician" under applicable New York and federal law.[10] As such, his professional decisions about Diane's "hospice care" legally superseded those of any of the hospice care workers—the medical director, the nurses, or counseling staff.

Dr. Quill suggests in his book that Diane "took charge" of her dying by asking him about how she might end her life "when the right time came."[11] He apparently refused her request for his professional assistance.[12] But Dr. Quill was, in his own words, concerned about "the effects of a violent death on her family."[13] He referred Diane outside the medical profession—to the local chapter of the Hemlock Society.

A week after this nonmedical referral, Diane telephoned Dr. Quill to request a prescription for barbiturates to assist her sleeping. This rather routine request from a home hospice care patient would not usually create any concern for the medical director, who must nonetheless confirm the attending physician's drug prescription for the nurses and others who assist the patient. Because of Dr. Quill's knowledge of the beliefs and practices of the Hemlock Society, the telephone request for barbiturates was a "defining moment."

Dr. Quill insisted on seeing Diane to discuss her sleep problems. He tells us, "[s]he was more than willing to participate in a superficial conversation about her insomnia," but he had to assure himself that she would not use the drugs out of despair. After some conversation, Dr. Quill became convinced Diane was not depressed and was, in fact, deeply connected to her friends and family members. He assured himself that she knew the difference between how to use the drugs for sleep and how to use the drugs to kill herself. With her agreement to see him on a determined schedule, Dr. Quill wrote the prescription.

Diane became a "case study" in informed patient decision making. She agreed to talk about her refusal of treatment to the residents in training in Dr. Quill's hospital. Apparently, from Diane's talk, or discussions with her during their regular meetings, Dr. Quill gathered the information about the events of the last three months of Diane's life. Prior to her death, she called her friends and asked them to visit for the purpose of saying "good-bye." Two days after her last office visit, Diane's husband called Dr. Quill to tell him that she had died.

Dr. Quill went to Diane's home and conversed with the son and husband about her last hours. He then telephoned the medical examiner— a state official—to inform him of the death of a "hospice patient." Dr. Quill stated "acute leukemia" as the cause of death. The medical examiner—the coroner—gave his approval for a funeral and presumably issued the death certificate.[14] As Dr. Quill writes, he told the coroner the cause of death was "acute leukemia" to protect Diane's family and himself from possible criminal prosecution for their respective roles in supporting her drug overdose.

Dr. Quill's deception had a larger public purpose: to create professional dialogue about his patient's suffering. He sought and obtained permission from Diane's family to write about not only her "case," but also about their own struggle and pain. He believed that as long as he protected her identity, no further suffering would be inflicted upon Diane's husband or son.

In retrospect, Dr. Quill seemed unaware of the institutional forces that could influence his prediction of no harm to Diane's family. First and foremost, he ignores the power and influence of the media as an institution. The editors of the *New England Journal of Medicine* may have seen Dr. Quill's article as an example of the logic of his "patient-centered" approach to dying patients. Newspaper reporters who read the press releases about the *New England Journal of Medicine* article in the early 1990s would more likely see a logical connection between Quill and the approach of fellow journalist, Derek Humphry. Humphry's bestselling book, *Final Exit: The Practicalities of Self-Deliverance and Assisted Suicide for the Dying*, provides his many readers with practical—and medically accurate—advice on how to kill themselves if the need arises, with minimal risk of criminal prosecution on the part of their collaborators. This book marked a noticeable shift in public conversation about suicide and even helped to spur some attempts at legislative reforms through referenda in California and Washington State.[15]

Medical "confidentiality" affords little or no protection to patients once a reporter and his or her colleagues obtain "confidential" medical information. As soon as reporters gave Diane a public persona, public institutional reactions were possible. When the local prosecutor—an elected official—became aware of both Diane's identity and Dr. Quill's role in her death, he convened a group of citizens—a grand jury—to investigate whether anyone should be charged with a crime. Dr. Quill was required to appear before the grand jury. This group of citizens, acting under their view of what New York law required, did not believe Dr. Quill's actions constituted the crime of "manslaughter," apparently because he was "not present" when she took her fatal dose. In other words, the grand jury did not think his act of prescribing barbiturates to a home hospice patient with insomnia was a culpable criminal act. Dr. Quill seems particularly surprised that his listing "acute leukemia"—what Diane apparently did not accept she would die from—instead of "barbiturate overdose" as the cause of death would create any legal questions.

Dr. Quill received a great deal of support from his professional colleagues during his grand jury ordeal. To them, the inquiry by the grand jury into crimes from "tampering with a public record" to manslaughter appeared outrageous if not "irrational." Dr. Quill's training in medical ethics did not prepare him for the possibility that some members of the community who vote in elections might point out to the elected district attorney some of the social dangers of Dr. Quill's admissions as a standard for medical practice. Those same social forces that encouraged the district attorney's response led the state medical licensing board—an administrative agency—to inquire as to whether Dr. Quill's conduct met professional standards. This body, consisting primarily of licensed physicians, did not find Dr. Quill's conduct in violation of professional standards of the state of New York.[16] Neither of these rather clumsy legal methods of determining "facts"—from the medical and scientific view of how difficult matters should be handled—led to any direct punitive consequences for Dr. Quill.

By now, Dr. Quill had become a "reformer" and sought to tell the story of how a professional relationship became in his view a "friendship." He justifies his incomplete disclosure to the medical examiner as a means of protecting the then-dead Diane from "an invasion into her past" and her body from an autopsy. He also tells us that Diane taught him how he could help those he knew well if only he would listen to what those acquaintances—those friends—really wanted.[17]

His book proposes that his experience with Diane provides an alternative to Humphry's lay person's guide and Kevorkian's careless infliction of death upon chronically ill patients. In Dr. Quill's view, Kevorkian lacked "emotional investment in his patient's well-being."[18] Similarly, Humphry's approach—while presenting accurate information about how to kill oneself—does not provide any "safeguards" against those suffering from depression using the methods described in his book. One can almost hear Dr. Quill remembering his patient/friend, Diane, when he articulates the need to avoid unregulated use of barbiturates that Derek Humphry's approach allows. The ethical metaphor for Dr. Quill's public policy on restraints on assisting suicide is the physician as friend.[19]

Quill expanded the number of patient stories available to his readers by publishing another book, *Midwife through the Dying Process*,[20] while his lawsuit to have New York's law against assisted suicide declared unconstitutional was being appealed to the United States Supreme Court. None of the nine patient stories of dying in this second book involved Quill's own active participation in assisted self-killing. In this volume, he more clearly expounds upon his theory that "good deaths" for patients require the development of long-term caring relationships with physicians. The essences of this relationship are a partnership between patient and physician with a pledge of "nonabandonment" on the part of the physician. The concluding chapter of his book is a series of recommendations for professional and legal regulation of physician-assisted death. Quill's compassion for his patients, the members of their families, and their friends is apparent throughout his captivating storytelling.

With more numerous Quill stories available, it is apparent that he shares two things in common with Jack Kevorkian. First, like Kevorkian, Quill believes that "planned deaths" are better than unplanned deaths. Although he puts the matter in terms of dying patients' need to deal with their worst fears about dying, Quill asserts that physicians must have an open-ended or unfettered commitment to dying patients so that they can plan their deaths.[21] The last case study in his book, the story of a man afflicted with Lou Gehrig's disease, describes another physician who is willing to turn off the patient's respirator on a certain date under the title of "Loving Assistance." The fact that the compassionate physician was able to accommodate as mundane a requirement or need of the patient to complete his tax returns before dying in the presence of his family and friends illustrates for Quill the importance of planning death.[22]

Second, Quill assumes with Kevorkian that law must validate medicine. He suggests in his sixth recommendation that ethical distinctions about professional care of dying patients must be "clinically meaningful."[23] He further argues in his seventh recommendation that a physician must be able to respond to a patient's request for death assistance without the external influences of law operating on the physician's conduct.[24] Rather, he prefers a "regulatory" scheme for any method of assisting dying, including voluntary euthanasia.

Dr. Quill believes a system of regulation of physician-assisted death— ethical guidelines for physicians—can be built on the model of the individual patient/physician relationship he had with Diane. His method of preventing what he calls "abuses" of the license to assist death is deeply rooted in the notion that all of modern medicine's problems are solved through refinements of the doctor/patient dyad. The "bioethics" movement in this country has been deeply steeped in the doctor/patient dyad as a point of analysis. Within that tradition, physicians were not, however, entitled to engage in "mercy killings." But if one constructs the patient's death as self-inflicted—suicide—then the goal of regulation becomes to ensure that the patient is making a rational choice. In self-help lingo, the patient who "rationally" chooses suicide with physician advice and supervision has been "empowered" to take his or her own life.

The difficulty with this model of patient autonomy within the professional relationship is that it assumes that patients rely primarily upon physicians for their notions of "healing" and "health." While it is true that modern medicine is the dominant—and sometimes the only—force in many individuals' construction of health, disease, and illness, others, particularly those with chronic conditions, rely upon additional sources to define their concepts of health or healing. Diane, for instance, may have relied upon members of Alcoholics Anonymous (AA) as well as Dr. Quill to overcome her addiction to drinking. Whether or not Diane joined such a group, the millions of people who join AA or support groups for individuals with multiple sclerosis, epilepsy, diabetes, or other chronic conditions represent a significant social movement: a desire to find support for healing outside the parameters of the medical system. This is part of a desire to find community and a new identity as a patient. When a person becomes a "patient," he or she faces an ethical dilemma. While modern medicine holds out the ideal of "restoring" the patient to health, the reality is that much of the success of modern medicine leaves the patient emotionally and socially transformed. Those expressing a desire to die within the context of patienthood are in the process of struggling with who they are. The severely burned individual who faces disfigurement and disability and the alcoholic both must be assisted in their decision about their new selves.[25]

Vaginal cancer—Diane's earlier encounter with patienthood—created not only the risk of death, but also the risk of infertility if she lived through the treatment. Over the years, an individual like Diane might have learned to live with being a cancer survivor, an alcoholic, and a depressive, and be an otherwise productive member of society.[26] But when presented with the prospect of undergoing bone marrow transplantation, she may simply have seen the prospect of "patienthood" as inappropriate. Thus, there is nothing particularly troublesome with Diane or any patient refusing lifesaving treatment. It is an option the law has sanctioned, but in a way that seeks to support the patient resolving his or her own ethical dilemma in the context of modern medicine.

TERMINATING CARE OR DECLINING TREATMENT

Through a series of legislative acts and judicial opinions over the past twenty years, law now provides physicians with directions about the legal permissibility, if not necessity, of respecting patient refusal of treatment. The vast majority of these statutes and judicial opinions proscribe legal procedures for implementing the ideal of patient choice when the patient is unconscious and thus "silent" as to his or her present wishes regarding medical treatment.[27]

Physicians have difficulty implementing the law's ideal of patient refusal of treatment. There is some evidence that many prior expressions of patient unwillingness to undergo a treatment, such as resuscitation after cardiac arrest, are ignored by physicians.[28] Despite these imperfections in practice, legal reform has thus far been informed by the question: What are the most effective means of implementing the patient's ability to terminate care or to decline treatment?

The discontinuity between a legislative ideal of "patient autonomy" on the one hand, and the reality of medical practice on the other, might suggest that there is a chasm between law as an ideal and medicine as practical reality. In turn, establishing these two as polarities might lead one to believe he or she must choose one or the other. But why, in matters of such enduring significance as death, should one view the matter in this binary fashion? With an institutional approach to death, the supposed either-or dichotomy between law and medicine is false.

The goal of the physician-led legal reform movement is to ask the primary question: Under what circumstances should physicians be authorized by law to help some patients kill themselves? Physician-reformers are first and foremost concerned that this question ignores the Dianes of the modern world; patients who are infused with ideas about individual autonomy, physician manipulation, and legal maneuvering epitomized in Humphry's self-help movement. These patients ask for professional assistance in dying. Most physicians say "no" to these requests, despite survey results indicating that a large number of them would like to say "yes" in some cases.[29] An affirmative answer creates a risk—however small—of criminal prosecution because states have not, except in Oregon, created exemptions for physicians in their statutes prohibiting aiding and assisting suicide.[30]

Opinion polls indicating public approval of some form of legalized physician-assisted suicide mean there is far greater public acceptance of physician ideas for legal reform than the lack of legislative action might indicate.[31] Turning these opinion polls into legislative action has one large obstacle from within the ranks of medicine: the American Medical Association (AMA). The AMA is opposed to the legalization of physician-assisted suicide and offers better training of physicians in modern techniques of pain management as an alternative.[32] The association is "conservative" on social issues, but has traditionally been the spokesman for the practicing physician's interest in the political process.[33] With public opinion polls indicating physicians overwhelmingly favoring legalization, the AMA's political opposition to legalization of physician-assisted suicide requires some explanation.

The AMA develops its political position, like all interest groups, in the present social and economic context. The overriding political concerns with medicine for the past decade have been costs and access. Within this environment of managed care and reduced government spending on health care, the primary political interest of physicians is to maintain their economic and social position in a period of declining income for professionals.[34] The AMA, as well as other special interest groups, seeks to maximize the benefits to its members in the political trading and compromise of our legislative process. Other well-organized special interest groups—some of those associated with the anti-abortion movement in this country—have an intense interest in defeating any legislative attempt to allow physician-assisted suicide. The AMA's opposition to physician-assisted suicide is perhaps a well-designed strategic use of its political influence: It is not willing to risk the ire of powerful special interest groups at a time when the profession's economic viability is high on the political agenda.[35]

The leaders of the AMA are not willing to challenge the basic question the legislatures have asked thus far. Within the framework of terminating or declining treatment, the AMA offers the public—future patients of all kinds—improvements on "patient-controlled anesthesia" (a method of allowing postoperative patients to self-administer morphine intravenously in controlled doses). In place of Dr. Kevorkian, with his technologies of pain relief that kills, the AMA offers the prospect of all physicians trained in the latest and best methods of pain relief modern medicine and science can produce with the full expectation that managed care organizations and the government will be willing to pay for this innovation in medical practice.[36] Future patients will merely have to say "yes" to their doctors' offer of pain relief to have a "death with dignity." The AMA's opposition to physician-assisted suicide allows it to embrace the Hippocratic oath as a means of asking for the public's trust in the ongoing political, economic, and social debate about rising health care costs and the lack of access for many.

Legislators are not the only individuals who resist legal changes that Quill believes are in the public's and physicians' interests. Fellow physicians, the leaders of the AMA, are apparently just as myopic. At the same time, respected medical physician/writers such as Quill offer assurances to patients that their physician "friends" might provide them with the lethal dose if they just ask. Those who believe law should be understood on the model of modern science[37] find the clandestine nature of this practice unacceptable. Whatever modern physicians find rational and ethically acceptable should be adopted by law, not practiced furtively and with trepidation.

THE COMMISSION SAYS "NO"

After Dr. Quill's encounters with the legal system, the New York State Task Force on Life and Law decided to consider the question of legalizing physician-assisted suicide and euthanasia. This group of citizens under the leadership of the commissioner of health had been formed by the governor in 1985 to develop public policies regarding a host of issues arising as a result of medical advances. Its twenty-five members include prominent physicians, lawyers, nurses, philosophers, and representatives from public interest groups, as well as clerics from Protestant, Catholic, and Jewish religions. Some of the task force's previous reports to the legislature had resulted in specific legislative proposals regarding surrogate parenting, do-not-resuscitate orders, and appointment of a health care agent. These recommendations were eventually enacted into law in New York State.

The State Board for Medical Conduct in New York had urged the task force to provide some guidance to the legislature after it had found Dr. Quill was innocent of the charge of professional misconduct in Diane's case.[38] The three-person panel writing the opinion in Quill's case had concluded that he could not have been certain that the patient would have used the barbiturates to kill herself. The patient's failure to follow the doctor's orders did not make him culpable for her acts.[39] The purpose of this line of reasoning was to convince the task force members that the Quill case raised "important moral and social issues."

The members of the task force, however, understood that as a kind of state-level "commission," its public function went far beyond Dr. Quill's individual moral dilemma. As somewhat experienced participants in the political process, the commission immediately framed the question in its larger social context, focusing on the attempts to legalize assisted suicide and euthanasia in other states and the Netherlands, and on the manner in which medicine handled pain and depression. Within this framework, the commission recommended no changes in New York's law prohibiting assisted suicide, but did recommend changes regarding the use of pain medicine, including derivatives of opium, to ensure their availability in medical settings. Modifications of the maze of regulation of "controlled substances" might include removing the requirement that health care professionals report "addicts" and "habitual users" to the Department of Health.[40]

When the diverse group of task force members looked at the issue of suffering patients, it saw barriers—legal and others—to the effective use of pain relief for patients. In other words, the physician-reformers were seeking to change the wrong laws—those making assisting suicide a crime. The task force sought to give voice to another group of physicians—those who saw the laws and regulations regarding controlled substances as inappropriate inhibitors of physicians' ability to relieve patient suffering and pain. As a long-term functioning group within the political process, the task force understood that the price of allowing for more medical use of drugs for pain relief was public assurance that physicians followed the general injunction: Do Not Kill. The task force was able to reach its political decision *without* all of its members sharing a belief that physician-assisted suicide is inherently unethical.[41]

This social perspective that allows for a diversity of beliefs about the ethical appropriateness of a physician's actions in an individual case is anathema to the physician-reformers. Underlying their attempts to influence public policy is the unspoken belief that individual physician decision making—clinical decision making—must be the key factor in law's formulations. Quill, for instance, had joined other colleagues in proposing those clinical guidelines that could be enacted into regulations and statutes.[42] In an editorial in the *New York Times*, Quill explained that he decided to take his case of reform to the courts in the form of a constitutional challenge to New York laws against assisting suicide when the New York task force failed to recommend legislative relief.[43] Quill's frustration with the political process on the specific issue of legalizing physician-assisted suicide is symptomatic of a frustration with a process that regulates the dispensing of death by physicians.

"PRESERVING LIFE": DEATH IN THE REGULATORY STATE

After the *Cruzan* case[44] in 1990, the New York legislature enacted the Health Care Proxy Law. This statute authorizes adults to appoint someone to make health care decisions in the event of the person's incapacity. It requires that a future patient make positive choices to indicate that his or her health care agent can remove food and hydration—the matter litigated in *Cruzan*. The legislation was implemented by the state's Department of Health so that a person could execute the appropriate form without consulting a lawyer. The department even provided a printed description of the law and its requirements, a sample form for creating a health care proxy, and instructions about giving the signed form to appropriate individuals. New York, the state in which Dr. Quill practices, illustrates the complex legal process necessary to establish patient autonomy within medicine.

Despite the passage of statutes giving patients legislative rights to prevent the imposition of life-sustaining treatment, many fail to comply with the procedural requirements of exercising their rights. Lack of knowledge of the existence of these types of laws might be one explanation of why future patients do not seize what was thought of as important "rights." A more likely explanation is that most people may not yet believe that how they die is really a matter they want solved by the clumsy mechanism of law. Many people, for instance, fail to make regular wills before dying. Matters of life and death may be crucial to physicians, but may not be as high on individuals' personal agendas as media attention to Quill or Kevorkian might suggest.

Also, these statutes by necessity use legal categories—products of other statutes and courts cases—rather than the bumper sticker icons that attract popular attention. The statutory language which appears ambiguous to a physician—such as requiring that the health care agent have "reasonable knowledge" of the incompetent principal's wishes—is simply the product of the compromise inherent in a political process seeking to accommodate conflicting goals. In the legislature's attempts to deal with the generality of cases, some particular situations are left to judicial and professional resolution by any legislative enactment.

Interpretation of legislation—How does this piece of legislation proscribe my client's behavior?—is a question practicing lawyers resolve every day. In our present political climate regarding medicine, these questions of interpretation sometimes raise matters of public policy and thus illustrate the contours of our debate about physicians' roles in our deaths. When a conflict occurs between physicians and patients about the nature of dying, there are a host of laws or legal doctrines that might be used to try to influence court interpretation even as the adjudication skews our understanding of the "facts."

In a recent case, *In the Matter of Baby K*, a mother and her child's treating physicians were unable to agree on the course of treatment.[45] The newborn was permanently unconscious and had difficulty breathing after its birth. The attending physicians provided mechanical respiratory support and confirmed what had been suspected following the birth: The child was born anencephalic—with a major portion of its brain, skull, and scalp missing.[46] From the physicians' perspective, the newborn was "terminal" at birth. They wanted the mother to agree that the child's breathing should not be assisted, if the need were to arise again. The mother refused, and the hospital brought a lawsuit on behalf of the physicians. They sought to frame the issue for the court in terms of whether physicians are legally obligated to provide emergency treatment to terminal infants. They asked the court to interpret a federal statute on emergency medical treatment as inapplicable to situations in which hospitals' health care professionals have already provided food, hydration, and warmth to a child born anencephalic.[47] The mother opposed the lawsuit. Her lawyer offered another interpretation of the federal statute. Whenever the mother requested breathing assistance for the infant as an emergency patient, the federal statute required the health care professionals at the hospital to provide the child with a respirator. The trial court and the federal appeals court agreed with the mother's interpretation.

In arriving at its interpretation, the appellate court articulated the popular conception of Congress's purpose in enacting the Emergency Medical Treatment and Active Labor Act (EMTALA). According to the court, some hospitals avoided providing care to indigent patients by either refusing emergency treatment or transferring them to public hospitals before their conditions had stabilized.[48] The EMTALA requires all hospitals receiving federal Medicare or Medicaid funds to have appropriate medical screening procedures in their emergency rooms.[49] If this screening process reveals a medical emergency, the hospital must treat the patient to the point of stabilization or provide for transfer of the patient to an appropriate facility.[50] This procedure is to be used on all incoming patients.

Since the hospital had unsuccessfully tried to transfer Baby K to another hospital when the dispute with the mother arose, the main point of contention was the meaning of "stabilization." The hospital argued that the federal court should consider the language of a state statute indicating that courts should not construe that state statute "to require a physician to prescribe or render medical treatment to a patient that the physician determines to be medically or ethically inappropriate."[51] Under this view, the child's underlying anencephalic condition meant her stable medical condition was "terminal," and respiratory care on an emergency basis was inappropriate.

The court rejected this argument, but the appellate judge writing the opinion was not insensitive to the dilemma in which the physicians found themselves. He only suggested that any relief must come through legislative action. The dissenting judge's only disagreement with the majority opinion was over whether the legislature authorized the judiciary to decide on a case-by-case basis the meaning of stabilization. The dissent's reasoning, however, shifts the institutional balance towards courts and away from legislatures. In effect, the dissent attempts to protect medicine from the political forces without telling us why this exemption should exist.

This case makes us wonder if Congress saw a flaw in the system of medicine and in particular the manner in which hospitals and physicians approach "costly patients." The dissent assumes that courts are the appropriate institution to handle all conflicts such as those that might arise when the mother and father disagree about the treatment of their hospitalized newborn, as was in fact the situation in this case. In its desire to protect physicians' interest in its definition of "medical futility,"[52] the dissent may not realize that in some of these cases of parental conflict over the course of treatment for their child, the court's posture should be to not decide. Not deciding is a way in which a court respects the institution of the family when it encounters the real-world complexities in the universe of medicine.

The result in the *Baby K* case is correct, because it avoids a decision that allows medicine to impose its view of death or "terminal" on a particular family. The court also avoids the apparent conflict between the newborn's parents by using one of adjudication's strengths and weaknesses: The court can only decide the case before it, and apparently none of the parties asked the federal court to decide that point. Pursuit of the litigation is important to the hospital and its physicians because the case epitomized how death has become tied up in bureaucratic regulation when the concept of "medical futility" had not been validated by the political process.

Despite the supposed commitment of law to "preserving life," courts have been in the forefront of delineating the circumstances when patients may decline medical treatment. Ever since Karen Ann Quinlan's parents had to go to court to remove her respirator in 1976, courts, by and large, have allowed relatives to remove life-sustaining medical technologies when patients were in comas or persistent vegetative states. Legislatures have not been silent during this adjudication over an alleged "right to die." Rather, they have provided more precise regulatory schemes for when physicians can be acknowledged to be part of the death-dispensing process of patients unable to speak. Until the 1990s, legislatures that authorized the removal or refusal of treatment did so in the context of criminal prohibitions against "mercy killings."[53]

CONCLUSION

Physicians have played a significant role in shifting public conversation about suicide away from a concern with premature death (particularly of teenagers and young adults) towards the linkage of self-killing by patients in need of physician help. To do so, physician-reformers have abandoned the image of the physician as technician or fighter against death, and adopted the image of the physician as a possible friend.

The physician as friend confuses the very public role of modern physicians with the very private role that friends and other intimates play in individuals' lives. This model of patient and physician autonomy seeks to re-frame the legal question usually asked about death in the medical context. Rather than ask under what circumstances should legislatures instruct physicians to honor patients' wishes to decline or withdraw treatment, physician-reformers want legislatures to consider under what circumstances physicians should be immune from legal consequences for responding to patient requests for assistance in dying.

The refusal of political groups to respond favorably to physicians' requests for legal relief encouraged physicians to see constitutional litigation as the only solution to their ethical dilemmas. This "no" makes all the complex regulation surrounding death in the medical context appear irrational to physician-reformers. Law's interest in preserving life means suicide will always have a socially ambiguous meaning. On the other hand, physicians, seeking perhaps to become our modern-day secular priests, have sought to elevate suicide in the medical context to a highly valued blessing.

The larger difficulty is that medical and legal definitions are often conflicting constructions of the same social events. A "terminal patient" from a medical perspective may be from law's perspective a "child" with "parents" unwilling to consent to the withdrawal of treatment. While law may seek to maximize parental health care decision making on behalf of their children, the notion of parental control is not without limits. Neither is the notion that regulatory agencies can pursue the goal of "preserving life" without regard to the rights of parents to decide. Sometimes courts must interpret whether legislation authorizes administrative agencies to interfere with parent and physician decisions to discontinue treatment of newborns.[54]

Allowing the legislatures a prominent role in public policymaking over physician-assisted death encourages society to consider what is the best institutional arrangement between families, medicine, and law at the time of death. The political process, while not perfect, helps ensure that in questions of "life" or "death," more physicians will choose life rather than death when at the margins. While this does lead to some individual hardships, the processes of law are complex and can lead to surprising results. Even under the Missouri statute, alleged as a barrier to Nancy Cruzan's death, it remained the framework which her parents used to convince a judge to eventually remove the artificial food and hydration sustaining her life. On the other hand, the Karen Ann Quinlan case, which started the modern "right to die" movement, was horrific in some ways. We should recall that it took ten years for Ms. Quinlan to die after the supposed life-sustaining respirator was removed.

In all the concern about individuals' control over their own future deaths, the past and current problems of access to any health care are almost forgotten. For some groups, passing legislation to ensure that one can say "no" to health care becomes a primary social concern. Federal law, for instance, now requires any hospital receiving Medicare and Medicaid funding to give all admitted patients notice of their rights under state law to refuse treatment or to sign advanced directives about treatment.[55] At the same time, more than forty million Americans worry about their ability to obtain any form of health care at all. It is time to ponder the ways in which money defines the nature of the institutions that shape our lives and our deaths. Will physician-assisted suicide become a factor that is used to balance the resources/access equation?

NOTES

1. Timothy E. Quill, *Death and Dignity: Making Choices and Taking Charge* (New York: W. W. Norton, 1993), 214 (quoting a letter to the editor of the *New England Journal of Medicine* from Stewart Kind, M.D., regarding Quill's first article in that journal).

2. Timothy E. Quill, "Death and Dignity: A Case of Individualized Decision Making," *New England Journal of Medicine* 324 (March 7, 1991): 691–94.

3. *Vacco v. Quill*, 521 U.S. 793 (1997).

4. Quill, *Death and Dignity*, 60–61.

5. Most courts had based the right to refuse treatment either entirely on the common-law right to informed consent or on both the common-law right and a constitutional right to privacy. *Cruzan v. Director, Missouri Department of Health*, 497 U.S. 261, 271 (1990). Other courts had specifically rejected the need for basing this right in a constitutional privacy right. See, for example, *In Re Storar*, 52 N.Y. 2d 363, 420 N.E. 2d 64, 438 N.Y.S. 2d 266 (1981). Since then, many states have codified this right by statute or administrative rule. See, example, Cal. Health & Safety Code § 7186.5 (West 1996) ("An individual of sound mind and 18 or more years of age may execute at any time a declaration governing the withholding or withdrawal of life-sustaining treatment.").

6. Quill, *Death and Dignity*, 60.

7. Dr. Quill graduated from the University of Rochester School of Medicine and Dentistry in 1976. He focused on internal medicine and psychiatry during his residency training at Strong Memorial Hospital at the University of Rochester. AMA Physician Select Records, 1995–1996. Dr. Quill is currently an associate professor of medicine and psychiatry at the University of Rochester School of Medicine and Dentistry (Ken Neuhauser, "Tipsheet: Death with Dignity," *Courier-Journal*, March 21, 1994), a physician at Genesee Hospital in Rochester (Lisa Belkin, "There's No Simple Suicide," *New York Times*, November 14, 1993), and a private practitioner in Rochester, NY. Dr. Quill had also been published in medical journals prior to the "Diane" article, including K. Rost, D. Roter, and T. Quill, "Physician-Patient Familiarity and Patient Recall of Medication Changes," *Family Medicine* 22 (November–December 1990): 453–57; and Timothy Quill, "Utilization of Nasogastric Feeding Tubes in a Group of Chronically Ill, Elderly Patients in a Community Hospital," *Archives of Internal Medicine* 149 (1989): 1937–41.

8. Quill, *Death and Dignity*, 11.

9. Ibid., 10.

10. Federal law defines the "attending physician" as the one the patient "identifies as having the most significant role in the determination and delivery of medical care" (not necessarily a hospice physician), and "hospice care" is defined as "established and periodically reviewed by the individual's attending physician." 42 U.S.C. §§ 1395x(dd)(3)(B) and (dd)(1) (1996). The attending physician retains substantial control over the patient's course of treatment. See *Harris v. Richardson*, 357 F. Supp. 242 (E.D. Va., 1973); *Ridgely v. Secretary of Health*, 475 F.2d 1222 (1973); *Brewerton v. Finch*, 320 F. Supp. 68 (N.D. Miss. 1970). Under New York State law, every insurer, hospital service corporation, and health service corporation providing inpatient hospital care coverage in New York must also make available coverage for hospice care. N.Y. Ins. §§ 3221(*l*)(10) and 4303(o) (Consol. 1996).

11. Quill, *Death and Dignity*, 13. "Diane took charge in a highly uncertain, volatile medical situation by going against medical norms and initial advice, and choosing a comfort-oriented approach where suffering was minimized but eventual death was certain." Ibid., 64.

12. He was aware of the professional controversy over the published account of an anonymous gynecology resident giving a lethal injection to an anonymous 20-year-old patient, "Debbie," who was dying of ovarian cancer. According to the article, the eighty-pound patient suffering from "unrelenting vomiting" had not eaten or slept in two days and, unresponsive to chemotherapy, was now receiving nothing but comfort care. Her only words to the resident were, "Let's get this over with." The resident told the older woman holding the patient's hand (presumably the patient's mother) that she would administer something to "let her rest" and advised the woman to say good-bye. The young patient looked on as the resident injected her with morphine sulfate, killing her within a few minutes. The older woman "stood erect and seemed relieved." "It's Over, Debbie," *Journal of the American Medical Association* 259 (January 8, 1988): 272. Dr. Quill has said that his desire to publicize his own experience was because other accounts in medical literature, such as this one, were so extreme as to be easily dismissed by physicians and medical ethicists. Quill, *Death and Dignity*, 123.

13. Quill, *Death and Dignity*, 13.

14. In New York State, the local medical examiner is obligated to immediately investigate any death occurring without medical attendance. N.Y. Pub. Health § 4143 (2) (Consol. 1996). However, "reasonable information" is acceptable in fulfilling this duty; written statements of sworn witnesses and similar investigative devices are not necessary unless warranted by the circumstances of the death. *Ehlers v. Blood*, 175 Misc. 72, 22 N.Y.S. 2d 1001 (1940). In Diane's case, the medical examiner most likely assumed without hesitation that Dr. Quill's statement was trustworthy and constituted "reasonable information."

15. His prominence in the actual legislative debates has diminished somewhat since referenda in California and Washington to legalize physician-assisted suicide failed to gain voter approval in 1991 and 1992, and he resigned his presidency of the Hemlock Society. Humphry, a former journalist, remains, however, a molder of public opinion through his new group, Euthanasia Research and Guidance Organization (ERGO!), and disseminates information about euthanasia and suicide from his World Wide Web site "http://www.efn.org/~dhumphry" and his many books and public appearances.

16. On August 16, 1991, the Board of Professional Medical Conduct voted unanimously that no referral for professional misconduct charges was warranted. Nicholas Goldberg and John Riley, "NY Panel Clears Suicide Doctor," *Newsday*, August 17, 1991.

17. He says that she in fact taught him to "take small risks for people that I really know and care about." Quill, *Death and Dignity*, 16.

18. Ibid., 124.

19. Justice Fried of the Massachusetts Supreme Court, when he was Professor Fried of the Harvard Law School, once suggested that one way of viewing legal professional ethics was through the "Lawyer as Friend" perspective. Charles Fried, "The Lawyer as Friend: The Moral Foundations of the Lawyer-Client Relationship," *Yale Law Journal* 85 (1976): 1060–89. This model was rightfully criticized by Edward A. Dauer and Arthur Allen Leff, "The Lawyer's Friend," *Yale Law Journal* 86 (1977): 573–84.

20. Timothy E. Quill, *A Midwife Through the Dying Process: Stories of Healing and Hard Choices at the End of Life* (Baltimore, MD: The Johns Hopkins University Press, 1996).

21. Ibid., 206–7.

22. Ibid., 179–201.

23. Ibid., 210.

24. He makes the following statement: "All decisions having such profound consequences should be made entirely in the patient's best interests, as free as possible of adverse external influences." Ibid., 213.

25. See generally, William F. May, *The Patient's Ordeal* (Bloomington, IN: Indiana University Press, 1991).

26. The novelist Reynolds Price described his own experiences of being a cancer survivor in *A Whole New Life* (New York: Atheneum, 1994).

27. Robert A. Burt, *Taking Care of Strangers: The Role of Law in Doctor-Patient Relations* (New York: Free Press, 1979), 144–73.

28. See William Knaus et al., "A Controlled Trial to Improve Care for Seriously Ill Hospitalized Patients," *Journal of the American Medical Association* 274 (Novem-

ber 22–29, 1995): 1591–98. The study, known as SUPPORT, examined physician-patient communication and interactions for several thousand critically ill patients over a two-year period. The researchers found that 70 percent of the patients were never asked whether they preferred do-not-resuscitate orders (DNRs), 53 percent of physicians did not know when their patients preferred DNRs, and 49 percent of patients requesting DNRs actually got them. The researchers then compiled an "intervention" group of critically ill patients, for which specially-trained nurses worked closely with families, patients, and their physicians to formulate advance directives. Still, "to the researchers' dismay," the patients from this second group were equally likely to have their wishes ignored. Both groups were then equally likely to spend time in intensive care units and die with moderate to severe pain. The researchers concluded that enhancing physician-patient communication is apparently not adequate for improving current practices.

29. J. G. Bachman et al., "Attitudes of Michigan Physicians and the Public toward Legalizing Physician-Assisted Suicide and Voluntary Euthanasia," *New England Journal of Medicine* 334 (February 1, 1996): 303–309 (35 percent of physicians said they might participate if requested—22 percent in either assisted suicide or voluntary euthanasia, 13 percent in assisted suicide only); M. A. Lee et al., "Legalizing Assisted Suicide—Views of Physicians in Oregon," *New England Journal of Medicine* 334 (February 1, 1996): 310–15 (46 percent might be willing to assist a suicide if it were legal to do so); J. S. Cohen et al., "Attitudes Toward Assisted Suicide and Euthanasia Among Physicians in Washington State," *New England Journal of Medicine* 331 (July 14, 1994): 89–94 (40 percent willing to assist a patient in committing suicide, 33 percent willing to perform voluntary euthanasia); M. T. Rupp and H. L. Isenhower, "Pharmacists' Attitudes toward Physician-Assisted Suicide," *American Journal of Hospital Pharmacy* 51 (January 1, 1994): 69–74 (34.3 percent of pharmacists willing to participate in dispensing prescription for physician-assisted suicide purposes).

30. See, for example, Ga. Code Ann. § 16–5-5 (1996). Enacted in 1994, this statute made assisted suicide a crime in Georgia and yet stated, "[t]he provisions of this Code section shall not be deemed to affect any of the laws, in whole or in part, that may be applicable to the withholding or withdrawal of medical or health care treatment, including but not limited to, laws related to a living will, a durable power of attorney for health care, or a written order not to resuscitate."

31. A poll conducted April 9–10, 1996, by the Gallup organization produced the results "Yes" (75 percent), "No" (22 percent), and "No Opinion" (3 percent) in answer to the question: "When a person has a disease that cannot be cured, do you think doctors should be allowed by law to end a patient's life by some painless means if the patient and his family request it?" Judge Reinhardt mentions a 1994 Harris poll reporting a similar number (73 percent) of Americans favoring the legalization of physician-assisted suicide in the majority opinion he wrote for the *Compassion in Dying* case, 79 F. 3d 790, 810.

32. Jeremy Manier, "AMA Affirms Opposition to Assisted Suicides," *Chicago Tribune*, June 26, 1996; American Medical Association, *Code of Medical Ethics Reports* V, no. 2 (July 94): 269–75 (physician-assisted suicide).

33. The leading physician spokesmen on assisted death are usually academic. See Sherwin B. Nuland, *How We Die: Reflections on Life's Final Chapter* (New York:

A. A. Knopf, 1994). Nuland is clinical professor of surgery at Yale University School of Medicine and the editor of several medical journals. Quill received support from the American College of Physicians. Neither is a member of the American Medical Association (AMA Physician Select Records, 1995–1996).

34. Legislative attempts to curb the rising costs of health care can have adverse effects on both physician income and quality of patient care. The AMA has acknowledged that managed care often puts the financial interests of physicians in conflict with their patients' needs. See American Medical Association Council on Ethical and Judicial Affairs, "Ethical Issues in Managed Care," *Journal of the American Medical Association* 273 (January 25, 1995): 330–35. Many plans try to make physicians cost-conscious by withholding a fixed percentage of their compensation to cover unexpected costs of patient care or by restricting their authority to perform certain procedures, order certain diagnostic tests, or prescribe certain medications. Ibid., 330–31. Although maintaining that physicians must always place their patients' interests in care ahead of their own interests in renumeration, the AMA did not hesitate to also call for limits on fee withholds and other managed-care financial incentives. Ibid., 335.

35. Neil K. Komesar, *Imperfect Alternatives: Choosing Institutions in Law, Economics, and Public Policy* (Chicago: University of Chicago Press, 1994), 54–65.

36. Dr. Kathleen Foley, a leading authority on controlling pain (see, for example, K. Elliott and K. M. Foley, "Neurologic Pain Syndromes in Patients with Cancer," *Critical Care Clinician* 6 [April 1990]: 393–420) has been quoted as saying that in addition to needing the support of physicians, family, and friends, "a compassionate managed-care provider helps" a terminal patient in pain. Paul Wilkes, "The Next Pro-Lifers," *New York Times Magazine*, July 21, 1996. The tendency of physicians to forget to include in their discussion the costs of the ethics of physician-assisted suicide ignores the fact that "saving lives" is not always cost-effective. See Einer Elhauge, "Allocating Health Care Morally," *California Law Review* 82 (December 1994): 1449–544.

37. Martha C. Nussbaum, *Poetic Justice: The Literary Imagination and Public Life* (Boston: Beacon Press, 1995), 85–86.

38. New York State Task Force on Life and the Law, *When Death Is Sought: Assisted Suicide and Euthanasia in the Medical Context* (May 1994): 4–5.

39. The Board of Professional Medical Conduct found that Dr. Quill did not "directly" participate in Diane's death. While this reasoning seems somewhat artificial, it must be remembered that at the time of his professional misconduct proceedings, Quill had not yet written his book elaborating on his degree of collaboration. He seemed very honest with the board during the hearing, and the book does not go into more detail than the article. In its three-page report, the Board of Professional Medical Conduct went on to say that it would not be good medical practice for a doctor to refuse to treat a terminally ill patient for insomnia or pain, even if he or she suspects that the medication may be used to commit suicide. Nicholas Goldberg and John Riley, "NY Panel Clears Suicide Doctor," *Newsday*, August 17, 1991.

40. New York State Task Force, 171–72.

41. Ibid., 140.

42. See Quill, *Death and Dignity*, 155–67; T. E. Quill, C. K. Cassel, and D. E. Meier, "Care of the Hopelessly Ill: Potential Clinical Criteria for Physician-

Assisted Suicide," *New England Journal of Medicine* 327 (November 5, 1992): 1380–84.

43. Timothy E. Quill, "The Care of Last Resort," *New York Times*, July 23, 1994.

44. *Cruzan v. Director, Missouri Department of Health*, 497 U.S. 261, 271 (1990).

45. *In the Matter of Baby K*, 16 F. 3d 590 (4th Cir. 1994).

46. The physicians recommended that the child be given food, water, and "warmth." They indicated to the mother that the furnishing of mechanical ventilation was "inappropriate" treatment for an anencephalic newborn. They asked the mother to agree that if the child developed future breathing difficulties no respirator would be provided. The physicians asked her to consider an advance directive—a "Do-Not-Resuscitate Order"—that would allow physicians to withhold all lifesaving measures in the future. The mother insisted that her child's breathing be assisted whenever she had difficulties. After this impasse, the hospital sought to transfer the newborn to another hospital. All hospitals with pediatric intensive care units in the area refused to accept the infant. A month after its birth, the infant no longer needed hospital care and was transferred to a nursing home. While in the nursing home, the infant was readmitted to the hospital three times because of breathing difficulties. Ibid., 592–93. After the second of these readmissions, the hospital, on behalf of its physicians, brought a lawsuit seeking to have a court determine whether it was obligated to admit the infant a fourth time in the case of respiratory distress.

47. The defendants—the child's father and mother, who were unmarried—took different postures towards the hospital's lawsuit. The child's father agreed with the hospital's position that using medical technology to assist the child's breathing was inappropriate, and thus not in the child's "best interests." Ibid., 593. "Father K" terminated a relationship with the baby's mother before he learned she was pregnant. The district court discounted his wishes for Baby K's treatment, ruling that he was at best "distantly involved" in matters concerning the child. DeForest and Duer, "Federal Law Protects Treatment of Anencephalic Baby K," *New York Health Law Update* 1, no. 4 (April 1994).

48. Senior Circuit Judge Sprouse, dissenting from the majority opinion, argued that Congress's only intent in enacting EMTALA (originally known as the "Anti-Patient Dumping Act") was to prevent this specific abuse. The judge cites *Brooks v. Maryland Gen. Hosp.*, 996 F. 2d 708 (4th Cir. 1993) and *Baber v. Hospital Corp. of America*, 977 F. 2d 872 (4th Cir. 1992), both involving hospitals which had allegedly violated the statute. Congress does not have authority to regulate hospital practices, but as the provider of funds to hospitals through Medicare and Medicaid programs, Congress used funding as an incentive to get hospitals to provide a different response to indigent emergency patients.

49. In order to receive Medicare and Medicaid funding, a "participating hospital" must enter into a provider agreement with the Secretary of Health and Human Services under section 1866 of the Social Security Act, which regulates the services for which the hospital can charge the patient, prescribes review procedures, and so on. See 42 U.S.C. § 1395cc (1996).

50. 42 U.S.C. § 1395dd (b)(1)(a-b)(1996).

51. *Baby K*, 16 F. 3d 595, 597.

52. Ibid., 598–599.

53. The New Jersey Supreme Court originally held that Karen Ann had a con-

stitutional right to decline treatment. *In Re Quinlan*, 70 N.J. 10, 42, 355 A. 2d 647 (1976). However, in subsequent cases, many states, including New Jersey, backed away from attempts to "constitutionalize" the issue. See, for example, *In Re Storar*, 52 N.Y. 2d 363 (1981), in which the New York Court of Appeals declined to base the right upon constitutional tenets.

54. See, for example, *Bowen v. American Hospital Association*, 476 U.S. 610 (1986). In *Bowen*, the Supreme Court found that the Rehabilitation Act of 1973, which prohibits federally funded hospitals from discriminating on the basis of physical handicap, did not require hospitals to compel treatment of critically ill infants whose parents had refused consent, nor could the Secretary of Health and Human Services force state agencies to adopt a specified complaint-handling process for such matters.

55. 42 U.S.C. § 1396a(w)(1) (1996).

_____ Chapter 6 _____

Physicians' Constitutional Rights: Relievers of "Pain"?

Calling something a right is an institutional decision.

Neil K. Komesar[1]

Disagreement about the nature of constitutional rights in our system of law is prevalent. For those who view the Constitution as a set of principles for protecting individual rights, the United States Supreme Court's opinion on physician-assisted suicide raised the question of whether our rights may be transferable. Do physicians need to be exempted from the criminal prohibitions against aiding suicide in order for patients to realize their sense of autonomy in dying? In other words, can the personal "right of privacy" survive patients' deaths in order to protect physicians from criminal prosecution, but not spouses, family members, or friends who might have assisted those deaths?

In *Washington v. Glucksberg*[2] and *Vacco v. Quill*,[3] the United States Supreme Court answered this question in its constitutional form with a "no" by affirming that criminal prosecutions of physicians for assisting patients' deaths remain theoretically possible. In *Quill*, the Court rejected an "equal protection" challenge to New York's assisting or aiding suicide laws. Chief Justice Rehnquist, for the Court, reasoned it is "rational" for legislatures to provide immunity from prosecution for those physicians who remove life-sustaining technologies from terminally ill patients in accordance with state law, while at the same time forcing physicians to risk criminal liability if they respond affirmatively to patient requests for lethal doses of barbiturates. In *Glucksberg*, the unanimous Court used five different reasons to find no "liberty" violation in Washington's statutory provisions against causing or aiding suicide.[4] In so doing, the Court indicated that the debate about the appropriate role of physicians in our dying should continue in other policy forums, particularly in state legislatures, regulatory agencies,[5] professional organizations, commissions,[6] and religious organizations.

If we follow the lead of constitutional theorists such as Professors Laurence Tribe[7] (who represented Dr. Quill in the Supreme Court) and Ronald Dworkin (who, as mentioned in chapter 3, filed a brief),[8] the various analyses of "liberty" in *Glucksberg* would frame the debate in various state legislatures and administrative bodies.[9] Such an approach assumes that legislatures and courts should analyze the question of physicians' rights in the same manner—that the Court and legislatures are essentially the same kind of institution, at least when it comes to addressing major social values such as how we die. This approach encourages legislators and voters to examine the Court's rhetoric about the nature of "rights" in framing and resolving legislative issues.

But legislatures are, in fact, different from courts. Both are legal institutions, but they have different kinds of procedures, and different kinds of constraints. More significant, legislators and their staffs are obligated to listen to all the contending views, even those that differ from their own views and principles about how law should structure patient relationships with their physicians. Courts, on the other hand, are obligated to decide only those cases litigants bring before them. As a result of these contrasts in constitutional adjudication, part of the Court's job is to determine which issues should be resolved by the Court and which ones are to be decided by other institutions.

I reject *Glucksberg* as a guide for building the analysis for the ensuing legislative debate. Rather, *Quill* provides the institutional framework for delineating the issues we face in legislative forums and other institutional settings. The institutional analysis embedded in the Court's equal protection analysis in *Quill* is easy to miss for a simple reason. The Second Circuit decided its case a few months before the Supreme Court issued a major opinion on equal protection, *Romer v. Evans*.[10] In *Evans*, the Court held that a Colorado constitutional amendment violated the United States Constitution. The amendment disabled local municipalities from enacting any legislation prohibiting discrimination on the basis of sexual orientation. The Court did so without finding any "fundamental rights" or declaring that gays or homosexuals were members of a "suspect class."[11] *Evans* was a signal that the Court was going to determine the claims of a "constitutional right to die" by viewing the matter as one of institutional choice. *Quill* is thus the starting point for interpreting the scope of legislative authority to exempt physicians from legal liability for assisting their patients' deaths.[12]

A particular justice's views on abortion, choice in dying, or family formation, for instance, are informed by how that justice makes the choice between courts, legislative processes, or "the market" as the appropriate forum for public policymaking. Each of the five justices writing opinions in *Glucksberg* and *Quill* posed different questions about institutional processes.[13] All justices concluded, however, that the legislature is the legal forum for defining which acts of patients should be characterized as self-killing or suicide. In denying the physicians' claim for a constitutional right, the Court also granted to political processes the job of determining which acts of physicians should be characterized as legally impermissible assistance in patient deaths.

Although Chief Justice Rehnquist wrote the majority opinion in *Glucksburg* and *Quill*, Justice O'Connor's opinion in *Quill* is of enduring significance for the subsequent legislative analysis. Her desire to permit future constitutional adjudication around issues such as pain relief for terminal patients indicates she has less confidence than Justice Rehnquist in the legislature's ability to control medicine. She wants the Court to be able to adapt to changing societal concepts of liberty without granting broad definitions of constitutional rights. Lest anyone assume that Justice O'Connor is inviting constitutional litigation, she asserts (rightly, in my opinion) that there were no legal barriers to the administration of pain relief medication in New York. My own view is that legislatures should encourage physician-assisted living by modifying any laws or regulations which inhibit effective pain management for all patients.

IS WITHDRAWING MEDICAL CARE AT A PATIENT'S REQUEST SUICIDE?

The unanimous vote rejecting the constitutional claims in *Vacco v. Quill* illustrates how the judges of the Second Circuit Court of Appeals misconstrued the constitutional issues. The premise underlying the Second Circuit holding of an equal protection violation in the New York statutory scheme was based on an assumption about the allocation of institutional responsibility. The Second Circuit judges interpreted prior United States Supreme Court cases as implying that federal constitutional courts rather than the New York legislature had the institutional power to declare that the removal of medical care was the equivalent of suicide.[14] The Supreme Court not only rejected that premise, but used the brief from the American Medical Association and other professional organizations to propose a different institutional balance between courts, medicine, and legislatures.

Is the Definition of Suicide a Political Decision?

In finding the New York statutory scheme "rational" under equal protection analysis, Chief Justice Rehnquist relied upon *Evans* as stating the appropriate standard for judging the physicians' claims.[15] When Rehnquist asserts in *Quill* that the equal protection clause "creates no substantive rights," he means more than simply that the various legislative provisions in question are presumed constitutional.[16] He means the physician-litigants had to demonstrate that the legislation put physicians, *not* patients, in an institutionally untenable position.

To reject the argument that physicians could rely upon the rights of their patients, Justice Rehnquist had to reject the rhetorically powerful brief of Quill's lawyer and reject its premises about modern medicine.[17] Professor Tribe constructed his brief around the suffering and plight of now-deceased patients. Tribe relied upon the declarations of patients who were dying of cancer and complications associated with AIDS to support his assertion that a patient "in the final stages of dying is not committing suicide when choosing to avoid only unbearable, consciousness-filling pain or suffering"[18] and that only those patients had a constitutional right.[19] In essence, Professor Tribe invited the Court to construct the cases in terms of hypothetical patients rather than in terms of his client, Dr. Quill, and Quill's colleagues.

In denying Dr. Quill's claim, Chief Justice Rehnquist's opinion relies heavily upon the brief filed by the American Medical Association and forty-five other professional organizations. According to the AMA, physicians generally distinguish between terminating life-sustaining treatment and intent to cause a patient's death. Thus, legislation which prohibits physicians from assisting patients' deaths properly classifies situations in which physicians "intend" their patients' deaths. Legislation granting physicians immunity from criminal prosecution when they remove life support properly categorizes such deaths as "unintentional." Furthermore, such removal demonstrates the institutionalization of the ethical principle of "respect for patient autonomy" in modern medicine. More significant, Chief Justice Rehnquist relied upon language in the AMA brief to assert that "the law has long used intent or purpose to distinguish between two acts with the same result."[20] The fundamental point of the brief was that the distinction made in New York law would help ensure that medicine would begin to address its inadequacies regarding pain relief.

Finally, the AMA brief helped Rehnquist dismiss Professor Tribe's suggestion that the Court could determine that "terminal sedation"—the practice of providing pain medication for some terminal patients until they are unconscious—made the prohibition of a lethal dosage upon request constitutionally irrational.[21] The AMA's description of pain management in modern medicine allowed Rehnquist to put this practice into a conceptual framework of consent by the patient, the intent of the physician, and the ethical principle of "double effect." In holding that legislative distinctions were rational in general, Chief Justice Rehnquist could acknowledge differences of opinion in medicine regarding physician-assisted death and the possibility of some situations where there might be a constitutional defect in a legislative scheme. But what establishes "suicide" within law is decided by political processes, not constitutional adjudication.

Once it had been decided in *Glucksberg* that the then-dead plaintiffs had no constitutional right to physicians' assistance, the primary question for Chief Justice Rehnquist in *Vacco v. Quill* was whether the New York legislature had somehow infringed upon physicians' constitutional rights. For Rehnquist, upholding the constitutionality of criminal prohibitions against assisted suicide effectuates the appropriate institutional balance between legislatures, courts, and medicine.[22] Underlying Chief Justice Rehnquist's construction of the issues in *Vacco* is an institutional choice of legislatures rather than courts as the primary determiners of suicide.

When Are Judges and Juries Allowed to Invalidate Physicians' Convictions for Assisted Suicide?

Justice Stevens's concurring opinion, in which he discusses the constitutional issues in both *Quill* and *Glucksberg*, presents a different view of the appropriate institutional balance between medicine, legislatures, and courts. He relies upon the briefs of Professor Tribe and other amici curiae urging the Court to find a constitutional right to physician-assisted suicide in framing the issues in regard to medicine, but ultimately rejects their constitutional analysis. By suggesting that constitutional questions might arise when the states seek to impose criminal sanctions for the practice of physician-assisted suicide, Justice Stevens in effect chooses courts as the appropriate forum for resolution.

For Stevens, the constitutional issue regarding physician-assisted suicide is similar to those associated with the imposition of the death penalty.[23] The Court has become the ultimate arbiter of whether the imposition of the death penalty is appropriate, since legislatures cannot constitutionally require the death penalty for all crimes or even all homicides.[24] For Stevens, the issue is whether the particular plaintiffs before the Court had, in fact, demonstrated the unconstitutionality of the statute when, according to him, none of the patient-plaintiffs or the physician-plaintiffs in the Washington case "was threatened with prosecution for assisting in the suicide of a particular patient."[25]

In addressing what is essentially the "due process" issue and the most relevant precedent, *Cruzan v. Director, Missouri Department of Health*,[26] Justice Stevens relies upon the brief filed by Professor Dworkin and his philosopher colleagues to assert that the state's interest in preserving life in general is limited by "the individual's interest in choosing a final chapter that accords with her life story, rather than one that demeans her values and poisons memories of her."[27]

In *Quill*, Justice Stevens refers to the brief filed by the American Medical Association in order to criticize its basic premise about "intent." He uses the practice of "terminal sedation" as described by Tribe to suggest that Chief Justice Rehnquist and the AMA's assertion that legislatures can make distinctions on the basis of physicians' intent is "illusory."[28] Justice Stevens wants the Court's door to be open to future constitutional challenges.[29] Chief Justice Rehnquist wants the debate about physician-assisted death transferred to state legislatures.

Are Legislative Decisions Not to Ban Certain Medical Practices Arbitrary Exercises of Legislative Authority?

Justice Souter's short concurring opinion in *Quill* adopts Justice Stevens's view that the state "permits" what he calls "death-hastening pain medication."[30] In his attempt to synthesize the Court's complex due process and equal protection cases through a "principled" methodology for determining the constitutionality of statutes, Justice Souter assumes that the question is whether courts or legislatures should "permit" terminal sedation.[31] He holds that it is appropriate for legislatures to "permit" the practice. He fails, however, to consider the empirical reality that the practice was authorized by the institution of medicine for two reasons.

First, his common-law method of adjudication assumes that "terminal coma" is what Professor Tribe described as opposed to the end result of a carefully thought through process of medical intervention.[32] As the patient is gradually given increased doses of pain medication, his or her tolerance for the medication grows. In other words, an ethical physician does not commence pain medication with the intent of creating "terminal coma." Rather, the amount of sedation for a terminally ill patient is arrived at after careful consideration of the particular patient's condition and in consultation with the patient and his or her family members.[33]

The significance of Justice Souter's framing of the question is that legislatures can make distinctions between various proposed medical practices without violating the Constitution. Yet, implicit in Souter's opinion in *Glucksberg* is the proposition that the Court holds the ultimate authority to determine if a certain legislative distinction is an arbitrary infringement on liberty. Within this somewhat complex methodology is an invitation to continue constitutional adjudication.

Does Medicine Cause Deaths Without Dignity?

Justice Breyer is more explicit about the nature of the constitutional adjudication which might follow. He asserts specifically that there may be some type of constitutional "right to die with dignity."[34] He relies upon the briefs of the AMA, the National Hospice Care Organization, and Choice in Dying to frame the issue as one of medicine's failures: "Medical technology, we are repeatedly told, makes the administration of pain-relieving drugs sufficient, except for a very few individuals for whom the ineffectiveness of pain control medicine can mean, not pain, but the need for sedation which can end in a coma."[35] According to Justice Breyer, state statutes or judicial rulings did not prevent patients from obtaining pain relief.[36] As he states in his opinion, many terminally ill patients do not receive adequate pain medication "for institutional reasons or inadequacies or obstacles, which would seem possible to overcome, and which do *not* include *a prohibitive set of laws.*"[37] Justice Breyer attempts to put a "gloss" on Justice O'Connor's concurring opinion which explicitly joins with Chief Justice Rehnquist's opinion. Justice Breyer begins his concurrence with the statement, "I believe that justice O'Connor's views, which I share, have greater legal significance than the Court's opinion suggests."[38] By joining Justice O'Connor's opinion, but refusing to join the opinion of Justice Rehnquist, Breyer implied that Justice O'Connor had a sharper difference with the chief justice than she stated in her own opinion.

Do Terminally Ill Patients Have a Constitutional Right to Pain Relief?

The portion of Justice O'Connor's concurring opinion dealing with *Quill* makes an important assertion: "There is no dispute that dying patients in . . . New York can obtain palliative care, even when doing so would hasten their deaths."[39] This assertion makes clear that the case does not raise the question of whether those terminally ill patients who are "suffering" can obtain pain relief. She strikes a different institutional balance from Chief Justice Rehnquist. And by framing the question in terms of relief of patient suffering, Justice O'Connor narrows the scope of any future constitutional claims. She shuts the door on a claim about suicide, but clearly wants to provide litigants with greater access to courts on issues of suffering during their terminal illnesses than Chief Justice Rehnquist's analysis permits.

I make this assertion because of her opinion in previous cases dealing with medicine. First, recall that she wrote a short concurring opinion in *Cruzan,* in which she made clear that she wanted to leave open the question of whether the legislature could prohibit a surrogate from removing medical treatment on behalf of a comatose patient. While there was no state in which an explicit prohibition against surrogate removal existed, O'Connor seems aware of the potential of other institutional forces such as religion or medicine to influence legislation regarding the removal of life support.[40]

More important, she indicated in *Planned Parenthood v. Casey*,[41] the most recent major abortion case, that she wants the Court to have flexibility in dealing with changing social conditions. Put more pragmatically, when she committed the issue of physician-assisted death to the "laboratories" of the states, she provided a context for both legislatures and potential litigants.[42] For potential litigants, she made it clear that "facial" as opposed to "as applied" attacks on regulatory schemes regarding the dispensing of drugs would receive a cool reception.[43] In addition, it is apparent that who the plaintiff is would make a great deal of difference in the outcome of any future constitutional adjudication. Thus, a physician subject to professional discipline for administering pain medication to a terminally ill patient might be able to raise the liberty claim of her patient to obtain adequate pain relief.

THE FEDERAL FRAMEWORK FOR SUBSEQUENT LEGISLATIVE DEBATES

All nine justices agree with Justice O'Connor's rhetoric about the constitutional right to palliative care.[44] As a practical matter, this implies that any legislation affirming a general prohibition against assisting suicide should have a specific provision exempting physicians who are administering palliative care.[45] Of course, Jack Kevorkian has been able to use a similar clause in the now-defunct Michigan law to argue successfully before juries that his use of carbon monoxide was meant to relieve the patient's pain rather than kill the patient. From an institutional perspective, we should distinguish what jurors are allowed to do by constitutional design, and what constitutional constraints legislatures might have. In other words, the restrictions on legislatures and juries are different. As a consequence, the state legislative debate begins by eliminating the policy option of tightening up pain medication regulations.

None of the major players opposed to physician-assisted suicide in the constitutional and political forums such as the AMA and Catholic Church have any interest in more restrictive regulation of pain medication. On the contrary, the AMA appears on record as being committed to improving patient access to palliative care. In this respect, Justice Breyer also speaks for the majority of the Court when he indicates that restrictive laws as opposed to institutional failures in medicine would lead him to arrive at a different result in any subsequent constitutional litigation over such matters. Despite Chief Justice Rehnquist's assertion that legislatures have wide latitude to define what suicide is, legislative drafters who wish to provide physicians with legal immunity for some assisted deaths face a new issue.

Shortly after the Supreme Court issued its opinions in *Quill* and *Glucksberg*, the Federal Drug Enforcement Agency (DEA) announced that the use of drugs for assisted suicide under Oregon's Death With Dignity Act constitutes a nonmedical use under federal law. This threat to prosecute the pharmacist who filled the prescriptions under federal narcotics laws could have led to another round of litigation. The attorney general of the United States subsequently ruled that the DEA's interpretation was incorrect. However, some congressmen promptly introduced new legislation to modify the federal statute.[46] So far, the bill has not been passed by either house of Congress, but symbolizes how federal legislation could enter the debate. Although the issue might be framed in terms of whether the federal drug law's definition of medical purpose "preempts" Oregon's definition of medical purpose, such a prosecution could lead to a testing of the parameters of the constitutional right to palliative care.[47]

Under Rehnquist's constitutional analysis, a state legislature has the institutional competence to define what is or is not suicide, and thus presumably what is or is not a legitimate medical practice at the end of life. On the other hand, Congress has asserted that federal funds should not be used to support physician-assisted suicide practices.[48] The actual implementation of any assisted suicide statute in the states faces two possible obstacles:

- whether the federal government's interest in controlling the distribution of drugs—requiring every physician and pharmacist in this country who administers narcotics to have a federal certificate—can override any particular state's political decision to have physician-assisted death, and

- whether the one state where voters, not the legislature, have authorized the practice of physician-assisted death can devise a scheme to pay for the lethal drugs without the use of federal Medicaid or Medicare funds.

Given that Oregon was the first state to attempt to "ration" its Medicaid expenditures, there may be enough voter interest in the cost pressures in medicine to tackle this problem there. Embedded in these questions is the larger, institutional one of Congress's role in medicine.[49] Proponents of assisted suicide in the vast majority of states, however, have an uphill battle. The Court's decision was in some sense made with full knowledge of the views of the various interest groups and that the very same groups were likely to participate in any political debates of physicians' roles in our deaths.[50] The Court's "no rights" finding probably has swayed the moral debate against mobilizing the kind of political forces necessary to overcome the inertia of doing nothing. In addition, proponents face a national coalition as indicated in federal administrative rulings and federal statutes or proposed bills, which are posed to place obstacles into the open legalization of physician-assisted death.

CONCLUSION

A patient's plea of "let me die" was recently transformed into the idea that law should protect the patient's ability to determine the timing of his or her death. *Quill's* rejection of this plea in its constitutional form means proponents of physician-assisted death must return once again to the legislative corridors. Once there has been constitutional adjudication, the legislative debate will take place in a different institutional context, where the political processes at both the state and federal levels must define their respective relationships to medicine.

These points are essential to consider in subsequent discussions:

• The equal protection analysis in *Quill* provides the framework for legislative consideration of physician-assisted deaths, because it helps highlight the role of the institution of medicine and its inherent limitations.

• Furthermore, any post-*Quill* and *Glucksberg* legislative enactments are constrained by a "constitutional right of pain relief" on the part of patients.

• Determining whether to grant physicians legislative exemptions to aid patient death is a function of one's view of the appropriate institutional balance between law, medicine, family, and religion.

The Court has determined that legislatures, as opposed to the federal courts, are the appropriate policymaking body to determine whether criminal sanctions, regulatory measures for assisted suicide, deregulation of the use of some drugs, or the inherent controls within institutional medicine are the appropriate means of responding to individual desire for control within this legal and medical matrix.

It seems clear that we need to refocus our energies as well as our vision and concentrate on what is, in fact, the real issue now and for the future. Pain management and relief are issues of life, not death. For most of us, as family members and as prospective patients, living the last part of one's life is central and critical. The more we know about effective pain management by health care professionals, the better we will understand the risks as well as the benefits of physician-assisted living in a terminal state. Effective pain management is important, not only for those who have terminal illnesses, but also for those living with chronic conditions. Whether legislatures should authorize physician-assisted death for those whose pain cannot be "managed" is the question the Court leaves unanswered.

NOTES

1. Neil K. Komesar, *Imperfect Alternatives: Choosing Institutions in Law, Economics, and Public Policy* (Chicago: University of Chicago Press, 1994), 43.

2. *Washington v. Glucksberg*, 521 U.S. 702.

3. *Vacco v. Quill*, 521 U.S. 793.

4. See *Glucksberg*, 521 U.S. at 728 (state's interest in the life of its citizens); Ibid., 728–30 (state's interest in treating the causes of suicide); Ibid., 730 (state's interest in the integrity of the medical profession); Ibid., 731 (state's interest in protecting vulnerable groups); Ibid., 731–32 (state's interest in preventing the "slippery slope" to euthanasia). Justice O'Connor agreed with the "vulnerable groups" and "slippery slope" bases, 521 U.S. 736. Justice Stevens agreed with the "preserving life" basis, 521 U.S. 738 and the "vulnerable groups" basis, while mentioning the majority's reliance on the "medical integrity" basis, 521 U.S. 748–50. Justice Souter agreed with the "slippery slope" basis, 521 U.S. 782–85. Justice Breyer did not mention any of Rehnquist's interests, but considered the lack of infringement of a right to palliative care dispositive. See 521 U.S. 789.

5. The Federal Drug Enforcement Administration recently announced that prescribing medication to assist a patient's death under Oregon's Death With Dignity Act would be in violation of its interpretation of federal narcotics law, which requires a "medical purpose" for every prescription. See Steven Findlay "DEA Challenges Oregon Doctors; Narcotics Law to Be Used Against Assisted Suicide," *USA Today*, November 11, 1997. The attorney general announced shortly thereafter that federal statute should not be interpreted to apply to physicians in Oregon. "Statement of Attorney General Reno on Oregon's Death with Dignity Act," Press Release, June 5, 1998. Available: *www.usdog.gov/opa/pr/1998/june/259ag.htm.html* cited June 10, 1998.

6. At the state level, the New York State Task Force on Life and the Law has been influential in shaping that state's law regarding the ethical issues associated with medicine. The New York task force report, *When Death Is Sought: Assisted Suicide and Euthanasia in the Medical Context* (1994), not only recommended no change in New York statutes regarding assisted suicide, but was relied upon by the United States Supreme Court in upholding the constitutionality of those statutes. See *Vacco v. Quill*, 521 U.S. 793 (1997). At the national level, over the past twenty-five years we have grown accustomed to legal bodies or officials asking blue ribbon panels to make recommendations about public and legal responses to ethical dilemmas in science and medicine. Public outcry in 1972, for instance, over the revelations of a forty-year study of untreated syphilis among rural African American males in Tuskegee was the precipitating event for Congress establishing the National Commission for the Protection of Human Subjects of Biomedical and Behavioral Research. Since that time, several prominent commissions at both the federal and state levels have made recommendations on policy and legal matters. The most recent example of what Professor David Rothman has labeled "commissioning ethics" in his book, *Strangers at the Bedside: A*

History of How Law and Bioethics Transformed Medical Decision Making (New York: Basic Books, 1991), 168–89, is President Clinton's appointment of a National Bioethics Advisory Commission, chaired by the president of Princeton University, Harold T. Shapiro, a distinguished economist.

7. As Dr. Quill's lawyer in the United States Supreme Court, Professor Laurence Tribe of the Harvard Law School, said after the Court's decision: "the Court, far from slamming the door, in fact, if you look carefully, left it open by a vote of nine to nothing." *NPR Morning Edition: Supreme Court Rulings*, National Public Radio, June 27, 1997. Advocates for the position that physicians' rights were matters of constitutional adjudication have focused on a final footnote in Chief Justice Rehniquist's opinion and language in some of the concurring opinions in *Glucksberg* to suggest that the Court may hold in a future case, with a different kind of plaintiff, that there is some type of "constitutional right to die."

8. Professor Dworkin, along with five other "leading philosophers" filed a brief on behalf of the physician-respondents in both cases. Brief for Ronald Dworkin et al. as amici curiae in Support of Respondents, *Washington v. Glucksberg* and *Vacco v. Quill*, Dec. 10, 1996 (nos. 95–1858, 96–110). Dworkin's views on the issue of assisted death were detailed in his book, Ronald Dworkin, *Life's Dominion: An Argument about Abortion, Euthanasia, and Individual Freedom* (New York: Vantage Books, 1993). For a critique of his framing of the constitutional issues, see Larry I. Palmer, "Life, Death, and Public Policy: A Review of Komesar's *Imperfect Alternatives: Choosing Institutions in Economics, Law, and Public Policy*," *Cornell Law Review* 81 (1995): 161.

9. Other "rights" theorists such as Professor Lois Shepherd are not necessarily unsympathetic to the Court's result, but nonetheless focus on *Glucksberg* and its implications. See, Lois Shepherd, "Dignity and Autonomy After *Washington v. Glucksberg*: An Essay about Abortion, Death, and Crime," *Cornell Journal of Law and Public Policy* 7 (1998): 431–66.

10. *Romer v. Evans*, 517 U.S. 620 (1996).

11. Ibid., 631–33.

12. After the Oregon Death With Dignity Act (permitting a form of physician-assisted death) was enacted, some individuals challenged the constitutionality of that statute on the grounds it violated the requirement of "equal protection." That attempt was unsuccessful. See *Lee v. Oregon*, 891 F. Supp. 1429 (D. Ore. 1194) vacated and remanded with instructions to dismiss, 107 F. 3d 1382 (9th Cir. 1997), cert. denied, *Lee v. Harcleroad*, 522 U.S. 927 (1997).

13. Justice Ginsberg wrote a concurring opinion, but she does not provide any reasoning. See *Glucksberg*, 521 U.S. 789. Her views are excluded from the analysis which follows.

14. See *Quill v. Vacco*, 80 F. 3d 716 (2d Cir. 1996), 722–23.

15. *Vacco v. Quill*, 521 U.S. 799.

16. Ibid.

17. Brief for Respondents, *Vacco v. Quill*, Dec. 10, 1996 (no. 95–1858).

18. Ibid., 5–8.

19. Ibid., 3. It is worth noting that Professor Tribe assumes that courts have an obligation to relieve the suffering of those patients. See Lois Shepherd, "Sophie's Choices: Medical and Legal Responses to Suffering," *Notre Dame Law Review* 72 (1996): 103.

20. *Vacco v. Quill*, 521 U.S. 773, 802 (citing *United States v. Bailey*, 444 U.S. 394, 403–6 [1980]; *Morrissette v. United States*, 342 U.S. 246, 250 [1952]). The latter case was cited and played a central role in the AMA brief. See Brief of the American Medical Association et al., *Vacco v. Quill* (no. 95–1858).

21. *Vacco v. Quill*, 521 U.S. 807, n. 11.

22. Ibid, 801, n. 6.

23. *Vacco v. Quill*, 521 U.S. 738–39, (Stevens, J., concurring in the judgments).

24. See Ibid., 738 (citing *Gregg v. Georgia*, 428 U.S. 153 [1976]; *Proffit v. Florida*, 428 U.S. 242 [1976]; *Jurek v. Texas*, 428 U.S. 262 [1976]). See also Larry I. Palmer, "The Positions of Justices Stewart and White on the Death Penalty: A Study of Two Perspectives on Discretion," *Journal of Criminal Law And Criminology* 70 (1979): 194–213.

25. 521 U.S. 739.

26. *Cruzan v. Director, Missouri Department of Health*, 497 U.S. 261 (1990) (upholding the constitutionality of the refusal of a state court to order the removal of a persistently vegetative patient's life support).

27. *Vacco v. Quill*, 521 U.S. 747 (citing the Brief of the Coalition of Hospice Professionals as Amicus Curiae for Affirmance of the Judgments Below, *Vacco v. Quill* and *Washington v. Glucksberg*, Dec. 10, 1996 [nos. 95–1858 and 96–110]).

28. *Vacco v. Quill*, 521 U.S. 751.

29. "[O]ur holding today in *Vacco v. Quill* that the Equal Protection Clause is not violated by New York's classification . . . does not foreclose the possibility that some applications of the New York statute may impose an intolerable intrusion upon the patient's freedom." Ibid.

30. *Vacco v. Quill*, 521 U.S. 809 (Souter, J., concurring in the judgment).

31. See *Glucksberg*, 521 U.S. 752–89 (Souter, J., concurring in the judgment).

32. Justice Souter's method of reasoning bears a close resemblance to the scholarship of the "legal process" tradition. See e.g., Harry H. Wellington, "Common Law Rules and Constitutional Double Standards: Some Notes on Adjudication," *Yale Law Journal* 83 (1973): 221–311.

33. When students in my seminar on physician-assisted suicide in the spring of 1997 questioned a colleague from our medical college about terminal coma, many of them assumed the question was: "Doctor, how much pain mediation does it take to kill a patient?" The physician pointed out that the amount of pain medication a patient can withstand depends upon the previous amount of pain medication she had been receiving.

34. *Vacco v. Quill*, 521 U.S. 789 (Breyer, J., concurring in the judgment).

35. Ibid., 791–92.

36. Some scholars have argued that the statutory framework governing professional discipline for misuse of pain medication needs to be modified. See, e.g., Sandra H. Johnson, "Disciplinary Actions and Pain Relief: Analysis of the Pain Relief Act," *Journal of Law, Medicine, & Ethics* 24 (1996): 319–27. But none of the litigants in the cases before the Court made a plausible claim of a realistic fear of prosecution or professional discipline for administering pain medication. The Court did, however, take up the issue of pain relief. See discussion of text accompanying notes 42–46.

37. *Vacco v. Quill*, 521 U.S. 792 (emphasis in the original).

38. Ibid., 789.

39. *Vacco v. Quill*, 521 U.S. 736 (O'Connor, J., concurring in the judgment).

40. *Cruzan v. Missouri Department of Health*, 497 U.S. 261, 289 (1990) (O'Connor, J., concurring in the judgment). See also Larry I. Palmer, "Life, Death and Public Policy," 168–71 (discussing Justice O'Connor's views on terminating medical care and abortion).

41. *Planned Parenthood of Southeastern Pa. v. Casey*, 505 U.S. 833 (1992).

42. *Vacco v. Quill*, 521 U.S. 737 (quoting *Cruzan v. Missouri Department of Health*, 497 U.S. 261 [1990]).

43. Ibid.

44. See Robert A. Burt, "The Supreme Court Speaks: Not Assisted Suicide but a Constitutional Right to Palliative Care," *New England Journal of Medicine* 337 (1997): 1234.

45. Several states' statutes prohibiting assisting or aiding suicide have an explicit provision exempting pain medication by physicians. See e.g., La. Rev. Stat. Ann. § 14:32.12 (West 1997) and S.D. Cod. Laws § 22–16–37.1.

46. *Legal Drug Abuse Prevention Act of 1998*, 105th Congress, 2d Session, H.R. 4006.

47. Given the debate about the "new textualism" in statutory interpretation, it is possible that the Court could decide this question as one of statutory interpretation rather than one of constitutional law. When the Court is dealing with Congress, this is often a different institutional problem than when dealing with state political decisions. See Antonin Scalia, *A Matter of Interpretation: Federal Courts and the Law: An Essay* (Princeton, NJ: Princeton University Press, 1997).

48. See "Assisted Suicide Funding Restriction Act," 42 U.S.C. §§ 14401–14408 (1997).

49. Note for instance, Congress's use of Medicare and Medicaid funding to impose standards about giving notice about declining treatment, 42 U.S.C. § 1395cc(f) (1996), and the standards for emergency room discharges, 42 U.S.C. § 12 (1996).

50. Bear in mind that more than seventy briefs were filed in the recent Supreme Court litigation. Whether a systematic analysis of all these briefs would indicate this was a case of "minoritarian bias" is not of immediate concern. What may be more significant is the fact that when the Court finds itself with limited capacity to solve a problem such as physician-assisted suicide, legislatures may find themselves incapable of resolving the issue. See Einer Elhauge, "Does Interest Group Theory Justify More Intrusive Judicial Review?" *Yale Law Journal* 101 (1991): 66–87. ("The same interest groups that have an organizational advantage in collecting resources to influence legislators and agencies generally also have an organizational advantage in collecting resources to influence the courts.") In this debate, Compassion in Dying, a nonprofit group formed after the defeat of the Washington Referenda in 1991, organized this litigation and was joined by other repeat litigators before the Court, such as the American Civil Liberties Union. The opponents had the likes of the AMA and various religiously related organizations, among others, as their constitutional allies. See Komesar, *Imperfect Alternatives*, 123–50.

Chapter 7

Physicians' Legislative Privileges to Assist Life or Death

Many patients would welcome the option of ending intense and hopeless suffering with the help of a skilled physician who can insure a professional approach.

New York Times editorial[1]

Now that the Supreme Court has ruled that legislatures can either prohibit or legalize physician-assisted suicide, the question is how they should decide. Because Oregon passed a measure in 1997 again authorizing a form of physician-assisted death,[2] the state may become the first legal "laboratory" for determining whether the hopes of the proponents or the fears of the opponents will become a reality. Proponents might look at the 60 percent majority vote in favor of retaining the 1994 initiative as evidence that many other states will follow the Oregon Trail. Opponents might attempt to file some type of lawsuit to block any implementation of the 1994 Oregon Death With Dignity Act, as they did when the initiative was first approved.[3] If, however, we want to take seriously Chief Justice Rehnquist's invitation in *Glucksberg* to have a true debate about the role of physicians in our dying,[4] there are some institutional lessons for the legislative debate we should derive from the Oregon experience.

First and foremost, even though the Oregon voters said "yes" to physician-assisted death in 1994 and 1997, voters in other states have recently said "no." In 1991, the voters of Washington rejected a measure that would have "decriminalized" several forms of physician assistance of patient deaths. Every interest group imaginable, from the Hemlock Society to religious groups, paid for advertisements to convince voters to adopt or defeat the proposed amendment to Washington's Natural Death Act.[5] In the end, this media-embedded political process produced a 46 percent majority in favor of the proposed Washington legislation and 54 percent opposed. In 1992, California voters defeated a similar proposal by nearly the same margin.[6] More dramatically, as noted earlier, Michigan voters in 1998 rejected a measure similar to Oregon's Death With Dignity Act by a 71 percent to 39 percent margin.[7]

Second, the initiative process for enacting legislation is a form of "direct democracy" limited to a few, mostly western, states. Although the initiative process has the same end result as the legislative process—an enacted statute—the legislative process is a different kind of institutional process. Some of its constraints—such as passage by two differently constituted representative chambers and the risk of gubernatorial veto in all states[8] ("vetogates")[9]—are not present in direct democracy schemes.[10] The interest group nature of our political process further constrains the outcome of the legislative process because on any given issue, many voters or nonvoters are indifferent.[11] Despite the media attention to the issue of physician-assisted death, it is not clear that most voters and nonvoters would necessarily place resolution of this ethical debate at the top of their political priorities list. As a result, when the issue is broached by legislators, the power of various interest groups to block the enactment of legislation authorizing physician-assisted death is probably greater than the polls would indicate. Blocking legislation only requires the institutional capacity to capture one of the "vetogates," be it the failure to move a bill out of committee or the governor's veto. As long as institutionalized medicine's political interests are represented by the AMA, its opposition to granting physicians the statutory right to assist patient deaths assures that such a bill is unlikely to pass in the two separate legislative chambers.[12]

Before the complex legislation granting physician exemptions from Oregon's assisted suicide statute, but prohibiting "active euthanasia" took effect, a federal judge declared the Oregon Death With Dignity Act, which had been enacted by popular vote, unconstitutional. His ruling prevented Oregon, at least temporarily, from becoming the first state to decriminalize some form of physician-assisted death. The decision was eventually reversed, and Oregon became the only state where physicians have a legislative privilege to assist death.

From an institutional perspective, the initiative process is an appropriate public policy forum for granting physicians legislative privileges to assist patients' deaths in a manner prohibited to the rest of the state's citizens by the threat of imprisonment. Constitutional approval of the initiative process does not mean that legalizing physician-assisted suicide is the appropriate public policy for exercising social control over physicians. Oregon's efforts to control the costs of health care by becoming the first state to develop a plan for rationing the health benefits of those receiving Medicaid is relevant to the public policy discussion of physician-assisted suicide. In addition, Oregon's legislation to provide means to effect patient and family desires to terminate or refuse medical treatment through its Living Will legislation is also relevant to the question of whether a regulatory scheme to control physician death-dispensing activities is good public policy.

PATIENTS' RIGHTS?

In *Lee v. Oregon*,[13] a federal district court judge issued a preliminary injunction preventing the implementation of the Oregon Death With Dignity Act in December 1994. The injunction became permanent in August 1995, when the judge ruled the act violated the rights of terminally ill patients to the "equal protection of the laws."[14] The crux of the complaint of unconstitutionality was the act's definition of "terminal disease" as: "an incurable and irreversible disease that has been medically confirmed and will, within reasonable medical judgment, produce death within six (6) months."[15]

The district court reasoned that the legislature's method of distinguishing "competent" from "incompetent" patients with terminal diseases was "irrational" when compared to other legislative measures. Under the legislative scheme for appointing health care proxies, an incompetent person has a nonphysician third party make a substituted judgment. Furthermore, the legislature has provided that those without terminal diseases who express the desire to kill themselves could be temporarily detained for examination by a psychiatrist or other mental health care professional under the state's civil commitment procedures. Thus, the notion of a terminal patient consenting to self-killing with his or her physician is not a rational way of protecting a person who is incompetent against self-destruction when compared to the legislative response to terminating treatment for incompetents and those who are viewed as dangers to themselves.

The district court judge's brand of equal protection of the rights for terminally ill patients is similar to the analysis used by the Second Circuit Court of Appeals in *Quill*. Both the district court judge in *Lee v. Oregon* and the Second Circuit constructed "classes of individuals" and compared the manner in which the legislature treated the various classes. But the two courts diverge in terms of the meaning that they attribute to the legislative provisions for health care proxies and establishing assisted suicide as a crime. The *Lee v. Oregon* judge viewed the initiative against the background of those statutes implementing policies of protecting a person from self-destruction. The majority in *Quill* used the health care proxy law as evidence that the legislatures allowed incompetent patients to kill themselves, albeit through the actions of a proxy. In *Lee v. Oregon*, the exemption for physician-assisted suicide was viewed as irrational precisely because it fails to protect incompetent terminally ill patients the way Oregon's Health Care Representative Act did. The *Quill* court found the criminal provision against assisted suicide constitutionally "irrational" because it denied competent terminally ill patients the right to kill themselves in an orderly, professional manner, the way that incompetent patients on life support could through a surrogate decision maker.

This form of "rights" based on equal protection analysis can be used by different judges to invalidate a legislative scheme in one instance that does not allow physician-assisted suicide as in *Quill*, or in another instance that permits such physician-assisted patients death, as *Lee v. Oregon* does. This method of discerning the meaning of equal protection of the law is very different from the institutional concerns expressed by the majority of the United States Supreme Court in *Quill*. There, and in *Glucksberg*, the Court indicated that political institutions could determine the degree of social control needed over physicians. *Lee v. Oregon* is striking in its lack of analysis of the popular initiative processes. This rights-based notion of equal protection does not seek to analyze whether direct voter initiative methods of enacting legislation should be the main public forum for resolving issues of how patients, their friends and families, and their health care professionals should be allowed to act. Objectively viewed, there is little to complain about in the process used by Oregon to create the first legislative act to recognize physician-assisted suicide.

REGULATORY DEATH

Oregon was not the first state to have an initiative ballot measure dealing with physician-assisted death. Oregon's proponents of physician-assisted suicide were less ambitious, and proposed an initiative measure which Derek Humphry, among others, described as having more "safeguards" against possible physician abuses than initiatives defeated in Washington and California.

The most important of these safeguards was a more restrictive definition of physician-aided dying than the one in the initiative that failed in the neighboring state of Washington. The Washington proposal, Initiative 119, contained two definitions of physician-aided dying: (1) a lethal injection by a physician at a patient's request; and (2) a provision for physician prescription of drugs for patient self-administering. Under the Oregon proposal, physicians were not authorized to assist mentally incompetent patients or those too physically disabled to swallow pills. The Oregon proposal thus excluded from its scheme the option of what has been called "voluntary euthanasia" and thus varied from the model act proposed in many states by the Hemlock Society.[16]

Other supposed safeguards in the act included the notion that a second physician had to confirm the diagnosis of the patient's terminal disease and mental competence; a requirement of a written, witnessed directive; the opportunity for physician referral for counseling; the requirement that the patient be a resident of Oregon; a waiting period between the oral and written request; and the actual writing of the prescription for medication for "ending his or her life in a humane and dignified manner."[17]

These various safeguards provided the analytical justification for the four "immunities" provisions of the Oregon Death With Dignity Act, "An Act passed by the voters as Measure 16." First, it exempts "any person" from civil, criminal, or professional disciplinary proceedings for participation in "good faith" in complying with the act. There is also a specific provision that allows a person to be present when the patient takes the prescribed medication to end his or her life. The clear import of this provision is to create an exemption from criminal prosecution for manslaughter for physicians, nurses, family members, and friends who comply with the procedures of the act in assisting a patient's self-destruction.[18]

Second, professional associations and hospitals are specifically prohibited from withdrawing licenses, membership, or practice privileges, from those professionals who assist patients' deaths under the act. Physicians and others opposed to physician-assisted suicide are prohibited from using professional sanctions against physicians who assist patient deaths. Physicians such as Dr. Quill would be immune from inquiry by the professional licensing board for his acts of helping his patient, Diane. In plain terms, a physician who assists patients' deaths is assured the continuance of his source of professional livelihood.

Third, the patient who requests the medication is protected from having this request for physician aid-in-dying considered as the basis for declaring him or her incompetent. This provision controls judges who must approve the appointment of guardians and conservators for those unable to manage their affairs or their personal well-being.

Fourth, the written request that is signed by the patient is not legally binding on the physician.[19] After the act, physicians are still free to behave in accordance with their own personal and professional values and ethics in any given patient encounter. Just as patients can always "revoke" the request for medication,[20] a physician has the discretion to decide whether he or she will write the prescription authorized by the legislation.[21]

These four immunities are legislative incentives to increase the number of physicians willing to respond to the request of terminally ill patients for lethal doses for self-administering. The safeguards mentioned above are designed to assure that the patient-physician dyads created are most likely to be "voluntary" relationships. But the legislature also used a form of disincentives in the new legal arrangements it created by establishing two novel forms of criminal liability.

First, the act makes it a crime for anyone to change or forge a request, or to destroy a recession of a request "with the intent or effect of causing the patient's death." This provision is best explained as a means of protecting the state process of death dispensing through the use of the threat of criminal sanctions against those who "willfully" interfere with the written instrument that makes the process operative or inoperative. Since the patient's death is a necessary result for the crime to occur, the penalty for violating this provision is quite severe: a maximum of twenty years in prison and $300,000 in fines.[22] There is also a legislative requirement that a judge impose a minimum of ten years for a person convicted of this "Class A" felony in Oregon.[23]

Further, it becomes a crime to "exert undue influence" to get a patient to sign a directive "with the purpose of ending the patient's life," or to coerce any individual into signing a directive.[24] This crime is also a "Class A" felony and thus carries the same penalty as the crime of tampering with a written directive for a lethal dose. Ironically, this new crime has a more severe penalty than assisted suicide under Oregon's manslaughter statute. This form of manslaughter is a "Class B" felony, which has a maximum of ten years in prison and a $200,000 fine, with a mandatory six-year, three-month minimum term the judge must impose. In theory, after the passage of Measure 16, a physician could not be charged with manslaughter for "assisting a suicide" of a patient in Oregon, but he or she could be charged with the crime of inducing a death request of a patient.

The new criminal provisions in a statute primarily aimed at decriminalizing physician-assisted suicide are a reminder of two inherent aspects of the political process. First, legislation is inevitably the result of compromises and never a complete "victory" for the special interest groups in favor of a measure. The proponents of Measure 16 included various Protestant church groups, politicians, and organizations specifically interested in "the right to die." Opponents included other religious groups, politicians, and groups organized to oppose the measure, such as the Coalition for Compassionate Care. Both kinds of special interest groups attempted to appeal to the voters, who were either indifferent, uncertain, or undecided about how they would vote in a popular election.

Proponents of Measure 16 wanted language in the bill to persuade those "on the fence" that their fears would be eliminated. Criminal provisions, which are probably just as difficult to enforce against physicians as the existing provision against assisted suicide, are a convenient tool of persuasion for proponents, since they believe the risks of physician abuse under the statute's procedures are quite small in any event. Proponents who drafted the measure deliberately "gave away" things to opponents in order to be more convincing to those "in the middle" who might vote for the measure or choose not to vote against it by not voting at all.

Second, our modern political process often uses criminal sanctions as "public solutions" to perceived problems without considering whether they are the appropriate means of social control. It is as if the political process has to believe that criminal sanctions, particularly heavy criminal sanctions, are an effective deterrent. We are one of the few Western countries, for instance, that allows the death penalty to be used as punishment for the most heinous of crimes.[25] Very little consideration is given to the possibility that less stringent sanctions might be just as effective as heavy prison sentences in deterring possible wrongdoers.[26] Nor does the political process consider whether new criminal provisions duplicate existing ones prohibiting homicide.[27]

However, from the perspective of the group most protected by the act—physicians—these criminal provisions are of far less significance than those protecting them from legal and economic consequences for their supposed actions of compassion. The important aspect of the statute is that physicians are given a legislative privilege not to be prosecuted or professionally disciplined for their death-assisting acts in accordance with the statute. In our post-*Quill* and *Glucksberg* world, the United States Supreme Court let stand the Ninth Circuit's ruling that this legislative grant of immunity is constitutional.[28]

RIGHT INSTITUTION, BAD POLICY?

The complexity of the constitutional mosaic does not mask the fundamental issue in the physician-assisted suicide debate: whether courts or legislatures are the primary public policy forum for determining the degree to which physicians are legally authorized to participate in patient deaths. Viewing the actual timing of one's death with professional assistance as a constitutional *right* conceives of law as a means of balancing the rights of an individual against the Court-constructed rights of the majority as represented in political decisions. The alternative conception of law views death as rooted in one's personal experience of family. A decision to change the relationship of families to the institution of medicine is primarily one to be made by legislatures rather than by courts. Under this alternative conception of law, courts—even the United States Supreme Court—operate in the same social universe as families, medicine, and legislatures, and bring to the physician-assisted suicide debate the inherent limitations of courts in dealing with death. These limitations led the Court to conclude that legislatures can decide whether to legalize or criminalize all or some forms of physician-assisted suicide.

From Rights Analysis to Comparative Institutional Analysis

The great "rights" cases of our times, such as *Brown v. The Board of Education*[29] and *Roe v. Wade*,[30] have spawned their own institutional lessons, which explain in large degree the present reluctance of the Court to create new "fundamental rights." Once gender and racial equity became a part of the political landscape, the Court's role in supervising race relations has shifted away from specific problems of schools to interpreting and thus supervising how far Congress and other political institutions can go in their attempts to "desegregate" the society.[31] Institutionally, this is a debate about how far the Court can go in its interpretation of the legislative language Congress uses before Congress will overrule the Court's interpretation of congressional acts.[32] The *Roe-Casey* development illustrates how the Court can maintain its institutional control over an important public policy issue without giving an individual an "absolute right" against political interference.

So, too, what we have thought of as the epitome of constitutional rights—Court protection of racial minorities—are now issues that require us to compare the social consequences of choosing various institutional arrangements. The racial narrative in our nation's history is unlikely to be swept away from any institution by a Court pronouncement. Rather, a variety of institutions—from universities, professional associations, private businesses, unions, local and state governments, Congress, and the Court—must confront their institutional capacities and limitations to ameliorate the effects of our own social, racial, and economic history. No one can doubt that the Constitution, through the Fourteenth Amendment, grants to the Court the institutional role of supervising the rules of amelioration other institutions develop, test, and use. But an honest Court realizes its limitations as the instrument of social change,[33] and is ever mindful that at certain periods in our history, previous Court decisions helped to create the racial divides in our society by denying Congress the power to prevent racial discrimination, or by allowing the executive to intern Americans of Japanese descent during World War II.[34]

Protection of a woman's right to abortion is, in retrospect, an enduring controversy within the Court as well as in our politics, partially because the Court did not initially articulate its institutional role in this important social and moral debate. We should remember that after the Court declared most criminal prohibitions against abortion unconstitutional in *Roe*, there were almost immediate political responses. Nearly every state moved quickly to impose some degree of regulation, such as making a third-trimester abortion illegal.[35] *Roe* was not a declaration of absolute rights; rather, it represented a shift in thinking about the institution of the family and woman's role in it.

Legislatures, Families, and Death

Most states do not allow voter initiatives as a means of enacting law. How then should citizens instruct their elected representatives to frame and vote on the issue of physician-assisted suicide? The issue must be stated broadly, to address not only vocal special interest groups who will lobby for or against some form of physician-assisted suicide, but also those many silent participants whose daily attention to this particular issue or politics generally is more minimal.[36] More important, it should allow for the possibility of the legislature doing nothing: either leaving in place the Oregon Death With Dignity Act legalizing physician-assisted suicide, or in another state, leaving untouched a statute criminalizing physician-assisted suicide. The question becomes: Have legislative acts or court opinions of a nonconstitutional nature achieved the right balance between medicine and families over when death should occur? Various legislators might answer that question differently, but if they are engaged in a group process, they ought to look objectively at their collective work over the past twenty years before responding to the pro-or anti-physician-assisted suicide forces.

Over the past twenty-five years, Oregon and every state in the nation has taken a combination of legislative enactments and judicial opinions to assure a patient's *legal* right to end or withdraw medical treatment.[37] Prior to the enactment of these legislative changes, some physicians, patients, and their families were terminating and withdrawing treatment. The legislators recognized the essentially private nature of these decisions, and used procedures as tools of control, such as two witnesses and restrictions on physicians serving as the health care representatives. The legislature avoided making a definitive statement, for instance, on whether food or hydration should ever be withdrawn. Rather, it provided procedures for this decision by physicians, the patient through advance directives, and health care representatives in the event of the patient's incapacity.

The legislators of Oregon, when contending with conflicting forces, had reached a certain political equilibrium: Physicians would be given legislative immunity when they terminated treatment in accordance with the patient's wishes as expressed by his or her health care representatives. Since these representatives are usually family members, families maintained some control over the timing of death. Conflicts that arise between families and physicians or among family members would be resolved within the public framework of law, which included what cannot be done: mercy killing.

Interest Groups, Popular Initiative, and the Institution of Medicine

The success of Measure 16, which allowed a form of "mercy killing" in Oregon, illustrates the institutional power of medicine. Physicians themselves did not have to act as a special interest group to achieve legal immunity for lethal doses of barbiturates; rather, others infused with medicine's vision of a life without suffering became the special interest group(s) to upset the equilibrium achieved through a representative process of enacting legislation.

By 1994, the Hemlock Society and others realized that a direct appeal to voters could shift the focus of the debate to the authority of physicians under the rubric of individual choice. By raising the question: Shall law allow terminally ill adult patients voluntary informed choice to obtain physician's prescription for drugs to end life?,[38] the decision becomes a direct appeal to voters to enact a piece of legislation. It shifts the focus of debate from the corridors of the state houses to the media campaigns that influence voters.

These campaigns might at first blush appear to be the best of all possible worlds: the "people" have the opportunity to vote on matters of utmost importance to them as individuals. But bear in mind that citizens are voting—making a public decision—about something they and their fellow citizens view primarily as private and deeply intimate. In our form of democracy, citizens do not vote on whether certain individuals should have children, whether they send them to religious instruction, or their relationships with their spouses. Why should the voting public determine the legal structures that might influence the way people die?

Special interest groups delude many people that they "ought" to discuss these matters with family members, spouses, religious or spiritual advisors, and physicians. For many, conversations about their future deaths are very comfortable, but just the opposite for others. The special interest groups that champion modern medicine's capacity to alleviate suffering also maintain its notions of "rationality." Those values that determine what is rational are connected to very secular notions of avoiding pain and suffering, and perhaps even death. Most people's sense of "family values" is grounded in the inner and social realities of the families in which they were born and the families in which they now try to live. Signing or not executing an advanced directive, for instance, is either rational or irrational depending upon one's own sense of family and the nature of our connectedness to others. One's attitude towards future suffering and pain—which is what voting on physicians' roles in our dying is about—is a function of not only one's present experiences, but one's religious and nonreligious spiritual experiences. The 50-year-old who is healthy may have a greater or lesser fear of future pain and suffering than the 50-year-old who has had a chronic condition most of his or her adult life.

For every Hemlock Society–inspired narrative of a "peaceful death," one can imagine equally "peaceful deaths" of those who let dying take its course in hospice programs or in hospitals. The story line of the Hemlock death narrative is the sanctity of the doctor/patient relationship. And many might desire some protection *against* the doctor-as-stranger who might be a part of our dying.

An alternative conception of the story of death is that the ultimate meaning of death is shaped by those intimate relationships people have enjoyed or suffered from birth to their impending deaths. Protecting an individual's right to choose or decline medical treatment has the potential of tragedy, because these many human relationships are at risk when people face death. But constructing law to maximize the opportunity for those human relationships requires a degree of social control over physician decisions.

In other words, medicine has become an institutional player in the politics of death. This does not mean physicians are necessarily a "special interest group" clamoring for the legal authority to assist patient death. In Oregon, for instance, the Medical Society took no position on Measure 16. (By contrast, the Michigan Medical Society was vigorous in its opposition to the Michigan proposition in 1998.) Rather, those infused with modern medicine's notion of the inevitability of progress have championed the view that law can create a world without suffering. I reject this vision: Law in either its legislative or judicial form does not have the capacity to end human suffering.

The main opponents of Oregon's Measure 16 are also institutional players: religious organizations. While these groups, such as the Catholic Church, have every right to influence voters, religion in this country is a private institution. Separation of church and state has meant that matters of how we view death, suffering, or even life itself are achieved without the coercive instrument of law or judicial enforcement.

Of course, the wall of separation in this country is quite permeable, but the public referendum over physician-assisted suicide in Oregon and several other states illustrates how important it is to our sense of community to maintain the boundary. The existing legislative privileges of physicians to remove even food and hydration under appropriate procedures maintains the correct boundaries between religion and law. In law, the person signing a directive or appointing a health care representative does so with his own religious or irreligious convictions in mind. To the degree that religion is important in an individual's death, the institution of the family is a proxy for religion if there are both legal procedures for withdrawing or declining treatment and the presence of criminal law for those who go too far.

Some possibility of criminal prosecution of physicians for "mercy killings" and assisting patient suicide remains an important boundary in maintaining institutional balance among law, medicine, and families. Legislative enactments, such as Measure 16 in Oregon, assume that law can perform a kind of laser surgery between the institutions of law and people's intimate and often conflicted sense of being a part of a unique human family.

CONCLUSION

Voters and legislatures in every state have the constitutional authority to give physicians a legislative privilege to assist patient deaths. This authority does not mean that legislatures should change the political equilibrium among medicine, law, and families. Legislatures, even in Oregon, have struck that balance by providing procedures for patients or their representatives to decline or withdraw treatment, while maintaining criminal prohibitions against assisting patient suicide. The fact that a popular referendum in Oregon recently disrupted this balance does not negate the fact that the public does not usually vote about individual deaths.

Medical progress can continue without legal authorization of physicians to become the relievers of suffering. Suffering comes from people being connected in positive and negative ways to others—from being born into a particular family that shaped, but does not control, their vision of living and dying. For death to remain personal, legislatures should not exempt physicians from the constraints of law important to everyone as part of the community.

NOTES

1. *New York Times*, May 28, 1994.
2. Kim Murphy, "Voters in Oregon Soundly Endorse Assisted Suicide," *Los*

Angeles Times, November 5, 1997. Technically, the voters only agreed that the previously passed measure should not be repealed.

3. William Claiborne and Thomas B. Edsall, "Affirmation of Oregon Suicide Law May Spur Movement," *Washington Post,* November 6, 1997.

4. *Washington v. Glucksberg,* 521 U.S. 702, 735 (1997).

5. Wash. Rev. Code §§ 70.122.010-.900 (1991). The ballot read: "Shall adult patients who are in a medically terminal condition be permitted to request and receive from a physician aid-in-dying?" William McCord, "Dignity, Choice and Care," *Society* (July/August 1992): 20.

6. California voters defeated a physician-assisted death measure sponsored by the Hemlock Society by a 54 percent to 46 percent majority in 1992.

7. 2,116,159 voted "no"; and 859,381 voted "yes." Michigan Department of State, Bureau of Elections, "Election Results, State Proposal—Proposal B—To Legalize Prescriptions of Lethal Medication to Terminally Ill," Official as of Tuesday, February 9, 1999. Available from: *www.sos.state.mi.uselection/results/98/gen/ 9000002.html* cited June 21, 1999.

8. North Carolina until recently did not have a gubernatorial veto. See Randall Chase, "Veto for N. C. Governor Tops List of New Laws in 1997," *Herald-Sun* (Durham, NC), December 31, 1996.

9. See Kay Schlozman and John Tierney, *Organized Interests and American Democracy* (New York: Harper & Row, 1986), 178.

10. See Jane S. Schacter, "The Pursuit of 'Popular Intent': Interpretive Dilemmas in Direct Democracy," *Yale Law Journal* 105 (1995): 107–76.

11. The 1997 Oregon vote on physician-assisted death was by mail-in ballot because of a recent provision of Oregon law allowing such balloting. See "Voting by Mail," Ore. Rev. Stat. § 254.470 (1996). The "cost" of voting to any particular voter was less in the 1997 ballot initiative than in the previous vote in 1994.

12. Some might argue that pain relief legislation could be passed because the AMA's brief in *Quill* indicated its support for adequate pain relief. But the AMA pain relief efforts might be directed at changing the profession rather than the existing regulatory and legislative structure regarding drugs. Or, just because the AMA uses the inadequacy of pain relief in its brief before the Court does not necessarily translate into political support for a particular bill.

13. *Lee v. Oregon,* 869 F. Supp. 1491 (D. Ore. 1994).

14. *Lee v. Oregon,* 891 F. Supp. 1429 (D. Ore. 1995).

15. Or. Rev. Stat. § 127.800 (1.01)(12) (1995).

16. Derek Humphry, *Lawful Exit: The Limits of Freedom for Help in Dying* (Johnson City, OR: The Norris Lane Press, 1993), 133–46.

17. Or. Rev. Stat. § 127.805 (2.01)(12).

18. This issue deals with the sufficiency of the evidence necessary for bringing charges and is not a question for the jury. See *Barber v. Superior Court,* 147 Cal. App. 3d 1006 (1983); Larry I. Palmer, *Law, Medicine, and Social Justice* (Louisville, KY: Westminster/John Knox Press, 1989), 99–103.

19. Or. Rev. Stat. § 127.885 (4.01)(4).

20. Ibid., § 127.845 (3.07).

21. Any physician who does not want to carry out the request is obligated only to forward a copy of the patient's written request to any new physician the patient selects. Ibid., § 127.885 (4.01)(4).

22. Ibid., § 127.890 (4.02)(1).

23. Ibid., § 137.700 (2)(d).

24. Ibid., § 127.890 (4.02)(2).

25. See William A. Schabas, *The Abolition of the Death Penalty in International Law*, 2nd ed. (Cambridge, MA: Cambridge University Press, 1997), 295–97.

26. Several studies have questioned whether increased severity of punishment actually results in greater deterrent effect. Rather, it is the degree of certainty of punishment which appears to be more successful in preventing crime. See, for example, California Assembly Committee on Criminal Procedure, Progress Report, "Deterrent Effects of Criminal Sanctions" (May 1968): 7; Johannes Andenaes, "The General Preventative Effects of Punishment," *University of Pennsylvania Law Review* 114 (1966): 949, 961–70; Franklin Zimring and Gordon Hawkins, *Deterrence: The Legal Threat in Crime Control* (Chicago: University of Chicago Press, 1973), 158–72.

27. For example, Oregon defines second-degree manslaughter, a Class B felony (maximum $200,000 fine and/or ten years imprisonment), as either a reckless criminal homicide or when "a person intentionally causes or aids another person to commit suicide." Or. Rev. Stat. § 163.125 (1995).

28. *Lee v. Oregon*, 891 F. Supp. 1429 (D. Ore. 1194) *vacated and remanded with instructions to dismiss*, 107 F. 3d 1382 (9th Cir. 1997) *cert. denied, Lee v. Harcleroad*, 522 U.S. 927 (1997).

29. *Brown v. The Board of Education*, 347 U.S. 483 (1954). While *Brown* may not have led to racially desegregated schools, its institutional effects should not be ignored. First, *Brown* allowed the Court to correct its own processes by overruling earlier Fourteenth Amendment cases that had upheld the use of race in legislative decisions that aided the post-Civil War construction of a segregated society in which schools, public transportation, water fountains, and even voting were defined along racial lines. Second, *Brown* played a significant role in shifting public attitudes so that "desegregation" could become part of the nation's political agenda. The 1964 Civil Rights Act and the 1965 Voting Rights Act have been amended many times, but have transformed our economic and social lives beyond the issues of race. The former has, for instance, had an enormous impact on "gender issues" in the workplace, education, and even the sports arena.

30. *Roe v. Wade*, 410 U.S. 113 (1973).

31. See, for example, *Bush v. Vera*, 517 U.S. 952 (1996); *Shaw v. Hunt*, 517 U.S. 899 (1996); *Adarand Constructors, Inc. v. Pena*, 515 U.S. 200 (1995).

32. The 1964 Civil Rights Act amendments are an example of this. See also Kenneth A. Shepsle and Barry R. Weingast, "Uncovered Sets and Sophisticated Voting Outcomes with Implications for Agenda Institutions," *American Journal of Political Science* 28 (1985) 48.

33. See, for example, Neil K. Komesar, "Taking Institutions Seriously: Introduction to a Strategy for Constitutional Analysis," *University of Chicago Law Review* 51 (1984): 366–446, 377–78.

34. In *Hirabayashi v. United States*, 320 U.S. 81 (1943), the Supreme Court sustained an executive order for an 8 P.M. to 6 A.M. curfew for all persons of Japanese ancestry. Later, in *Korematsu v. United States*, 323 U.S. 214 (1944), the Supreme Court affirmed the conviction of an American citizen for remaining in San Leandro, California after Civilian Exclusion Order No. 34 directed all persons of

Japanese ancestry to evacuate that area. In 1988, Congress passed the Civil Liberties Act of 1988 (50 U.S.C. Appx §1989a [1996]). It acknowledged and apologized for the "fundamental injustice" of the treatment of the Japanese in America during World War II, and authorized restitution of $20,000 to each living individual of Japanese ancestry deprived of liberty or property caused by evacuation, relocation, or internment.

35. Prior to 1966, a woman could only obtain a legal abortion when her life was threatened or, in a few states, when her health was endangered. But in response to the thalidomide controversy and the rubella epidemic, ten states legalized the procedure (in any trimester) when the child was likely to be born defective. These included Arkansas, Colorado, Delaware, Georgia, Kansas, Maryland, New Mexico, North Carolina, South Carolina, and Virginia. Ironically, after *Roe*, even some of these more permissive states criminalized third-trimester abortions. A few other states legalized abortion without reference to birth defects. New York, for example, decriminalized all first- and second-trimester abortions in 1970, with no restrictions whatsoever except that the procedure be administered by a licensed physician. N.Y. Penal § 125.05(3) (McKinney 1996). See generally Curt S. Rush, "Genetic Screening, Eugenic Abortion, and *Roe v. Wade*: How Viable is *Roe*'s Standard?" *Brooklyn Law Review* 50 (1983): 113, 120–25.

36. The number of people who actually vote in elections in this country is often considered a matter of great concern regarding the functioning of democracy. See, for example, David B. Magleby, "Let the Voters Decide? An Assessment of the Initiative and Referendum Process," *University of Colorado Law Review* 66 (1995): 13–46. On the other hand, if we consider that the present status quo might be "okay," the lack of active participation on every issue might be explained, especially when we consider how "taboo" death was as a subject just twenty or thirty years ago.

37. Oregon, for instance, in 1989 enacted its Durable Power of Attorney for Health Care Act to enable individuals to appoint proxies or agents for directing physicians how to care for them in the event of the person's incapacity. Or. Rev. Stat. §§ 127.505-.660, .995 (1989). Later, in 1993, the legislature enacted the Oregon Health Care Decisions Act amending the 1989 legislation. The 1993 legislation reaffirmed that adults have the legal right to make their own health care decisions and to appoint health care representatives. This change from durable attorneys to health care representatives eliminates some ambiguities created by the Power of Attorney procedures and made clear that this legislation dealt specifically with the institution of medicine, not the handling of financial and other personal affairs. Both the 1989 and 1993 acts contain provisions indicating that the legislature was *not* authorizing "mercy killing" or changing criminal provisions regarding "attempted suicide." Ibid., § 127.570.

38. Quoted in *Kane v. Kulongoski*, 318 Ore. 593, 607 (1994).

Chapter 8

Professionalism, Autonomy, and Medical Progress

To depend upon a profession is a less odious form of slavery than
to depend upon a father.

Virginia Woolf[1]

Americans have become so enamored with the idea of medical progress
that many believe physicians will soon unlock the mystery of why their
bodies decay and die. Through appropriate medication, personal train-
ers, and diet, they hope to maintain a kind of perpetual biological middle
age, if not the vigorous physical bravado of young adulthood. Until they
reach this medical golden age, they seek to overcome their fear of future
disability and dependence by appealing to an ideology of "professionalism," "autonomy," and "medical progress."

Within this peculiarly Western ideology, professionals and patients are
atomistic. Patients—unstitched from their own self-conceptions as sons,
daughters, parents, or friends—are the quintessential individuals. "Mentally competent" patients can weigh the risks and benefits of any
proposed course of treatment or nontreatment. Modern health care professionals' sole obligation is patient well-being. Science-based education
prepares physicians for continuous learning and innovation in practice.
Their own individual consciences provide penetrating judgments about
individual patients' needs and desires. In this scientistic world view,

everything is quantifiable,[2] and the physician-assisted suicide debate becomes defined in terms of patients' and physicians' "rights." Although the "rights" formulation has been rejected by the United States Supreme Court, emerging social and economic conditions demand new constructions in order to understand our impending deaths. Medical necessity has new constraints, and the issue of rationing health care has become a part of our political and moral dialogue.

In this constrained environment, viewing law and medicine as socially embedded implies that both patients and physicians have obligations. Medicine's continuous innovation in health care delivery services, including research on aging and biological decay, ironically creates an obligation of self-care for would-be and actual patients that has institutional implications: When are individuals morally *obliged*, but not *legally compelled*, to choose a nursing home or other form of institutional care? In this new ethical environment, law provides institutional support for the physician's obligation to serve each individual patient's felt moral obligation. The specific prohibitions on physician-assisted suicide are the social instruments for preventing the professionalization of death. The kinds of institutional structures that are in place in our society will have a great deal to do with determining to what degree physicians will be able to distinguish between their own professional judgments and individual patients' perceptions of life, dying, and continuity.

PHYSICIANS AS CONSTRAINED PROFESSIONALS

Even physicians now recognize that the fee-for-service model of health care delivery has given way to "managed care" or "managed choice." Managed care not only limits patients' choices of health care providers to those in a "network," but also the amount health care providers can charge for services. These organizational arrangements are built on the premise that "primary-care physicians" and specialists can provide cost-effective, individual patient care if there are budgetary limits or financial incentives for physicians to contain costs. This premise for organizing health care delivery is rapidly becoming the dominant mode in the United States[3] and poses a fundamental challenge to the ideology of professionalism and autonomy.

Private employers and government officials, the principal payers of health care, have focused on the growth in health care costs to argue that costs are "spiraling" out of control. Health care expenditures as a percentage of Gross Domestic Product (GDP) in the United States have grown from less than 10 percent in 1980 to more than 13.6 percent in 1995.[4] Proponents of cost containment use comparisons to other postindustrial societies to suggest that America could achieve the same or better overall societal health and spend a smaller percentage of the nation's wealth on health care.

An appropriate index of the overall health of any given population is difficult to determine, but if one considers both costs and infant mortality rates and life expectancy rates, the contrast between the United States and other industrialized countries is quite dramatic. Japan, for instance, spends about 7 percent of GDP on health care but has a considerably lower infant mortality rate and a longer life expectancy rate than the United States. The United Kingdom spends about the same percentage of its GDP as Japan, with a lower infant mortality rate than the United States. Our near neighbor, Canada, spends considerably more of its GDP on health care (9.3%) than Japan or the United Kingdom, but still has a lower infant mortality rate and longer life expectancy than the United States.[5] In this cost-conscious environment, patients and physicians face a formidable task in responding to the specific issue of how physicians participate in the entire process of an individual's dying.

Many commentators lament the "disproportionate" amount of health care dollars spent during the last few months of life. This complaint takes on a macabre tone in the context of a widespread public debate about physician-assisted suicide. Saving or extending lives uses what are now viewed as "scarce" resources. For the benefit of both physicians and patients, the public role of the physician needs constraints, particularly in the new environment where there is only one "pie." A 10 percent increase in expenditures on health care means a 10 percent decrease somewhere else, because a "balanced budget" becomes central to our view of our GDP and a political objective for both major political parties.

Rather than simply bemoan the evils of the "ethics" of the market, physicians should use the more constricted environment of managed care to reflect upon how their practices ought to fit within the larger social context. Patient-centered professional decisions will continue to be the ethical ideal in practice only if physicians take responsibility for creating systems in which economic decisions are made at the macroeconomic level—as opposed to the individual patient level.[6]

The physician-assisted suicide debate points out in dramatic fashion that the physicians' essential social role is to provide health care services for the many strangers they must necessarily encounter in their practice in a complex pluralistic society. Physicians will have to respond to inquires for assistance in dying, and may discover in these conversations, for instance, that they know less than they should about pain management.[7] They may discover that they must respond "I don't know" to some questions, without abandoning the dying patient. Laws against assisting suicide provide the background institutional settings for these conversations. Law does not—because it cannot—provide the kind of precise ethical regulation of what should take place within such encounters. Within the privacy of the family and physician relationships with nonhospitalized dying patients, there are many ways of navigating through legal constraints, as Dr. Quill demonstrates.

But the law does provide necessary constraints for the ethical professional. The possibility of a civil suit by a patient for malpractice on the grounds of "lack of informed consent"[8] provides some incentive for ethical physicians to respect patient autonomy.[9] The possibility of criminal liability, however remote, reminds conscientious physicians that their abilities to relieve "suffering" have some constraints. Even in a jurisdiction such as the state of Oregon that allows physician-assisted suicide, physicians are still constrained: at least one other physician must become involved in the physician's positive response to a patient's request for a lethal dose of barbiturates.[10]

Physicians should practice ethically within the constraints of economics and law. To do so, the physician must analyze the institutional significance of medicine by having conversations with patients not just about their dying, but also about their self-care. More "primary-care physicians" and fewer specialists—one of the effects of managed care—means physicians must begin to have conversations about the range of public health issues involved with the acts and facts of daily living in order to prepare future patients for autonomous decision making about their dying. Questions will always remain about costs for "heroic care" as end-of-life choices, but the question should be part of a dialogue that has begun within a primary-care context.

INCENTIVES FOR SELF-CARE: THE PROBLEM OF LONG-TERM CARE

Americans now realize that most of them will probably live very long lives. For those who feel connected to others—family members, friends, or colleagues—their deaths will always involve some sense of loss and moral questions, for which there is no medical antidote. Legalizing suicide in medical contexts increases people's dependency on health care professionals. But more important, legalizing suicide with physician help will not eliminate the ethical dilemma they face: What are their responsibilities for their own self-care?

It is now known, for instance, that scientists—not science fiction writers—are trying to understand the evolutionary aspect of longevity. The present generation of adults or their children may be offered "gene therapy" to arrest the aging of their bodies and their skins.[11] The medical benefits of the Human Genome Project will not be denied to those who need them simply because of some "fear of a world of individuals who are physically perpetually middle-aged.[12]

It is unlikely that legislation or regulation could stop the research on longevity now being conducted on insects, plants, and animals because related research in cell biology offers the "hope" for a cure for cancer and other diseases. The more likely prospect of a cure for cancer is an increase in the life expectancy of a person who is now seventy to from eighty-five to eighty-eight. The larger social question is: During a great portion of those added years of life expectancy, is one likely to be either partially or totally dependent upon the care of others?[13]

More important, do adults owe it to their children and the next generation to imagine a world in which they choose "institutional care"? The vestiges of rugged individualism and good health may make many scoff at those who move into total-care retirement communities. But once the option of long-term health care insurance is more widely available, many will see that nursing homes are not the only choice for them in their later years. They can also begin to see how incentives for long-term health care are aligned along a continuum of personal as well as public good.

If individuals start to focus on their own ethical obligations for self-care rather than on their "rights," they are far less likely to seek coercive means towards those who, for instance, eat fatty foods despite warnings from physicians. They are more likely to define "basic health care needs" so that individual variations are included, and to rely upon the persuasive power of science and medicine to achieve an optimal level of self-care. In other instances, the obligation is more ambiguous, and could arguably be seen as a matter of personal choice or liberty.

Furthermore, individuals are less likely to authorize that vulnerable populations be excluded from some minimum level of basic health care. This is why the law sometimes must be used to order state officials to provide heath care for prisoners,[14] and why there is concern and unease when politically constructed groups such as "illegal aliens" are denied health care benefits available to others in the community. It is also why medical professionals should consider the 15 percent of Americans who have no form of public or private insurance to cover basic health care costs as their special obligation. When one considers that the infant mortality rates in the United States for black children is 14.9 percent, compared to 6.3 percent for white children, one understands that the widespread preoccupation about "cost" masks other concerns about "access" and "quality" of the American health care system.[15]

Both law and medicine are social systems, but neither provides individuals with a universal moral system—nor should either be expected to do so, since such a system includes all acts of living as well as dying. Because medicine has become a part of our social awareness of how people live, 80 percent of Americans and their loved ones will die in institutional settings, but not because technology and machines have taken over "natural death." They might long to die in the familiar embrace of a loving friend or relative, but the morality of doing so is not as clear as they might like.

Recognizing that as they age they might have to choose institutional care, Americans have constructed the notion of "natural death" within medicine. This construct protects them from their fear of dependency upon others and their own lack of control. That fear of lack of control— their sense of alienation from their own sense of connectedness—leads to a strong social preference for a "quick" versus a "slow" death. The fear prompts many to search for a pseudoscientific criteria for professional decision making: One often hears, "She is *ninety-six years old*, why are the physicians bothering to unblock her intestines?" It seems counterscientific or irrational that the 96-year-old great-grandmother may have "demanded" the operation, despite the prognosis of a long recovery period involving nursing home care after surgery. For her, life is good, and she wants to maintain it. Without medical treatment, the intestinal blockage becomes the great-grandmother's "terminal condition."

Various forms of social and economic insurance increase an adult's sense of autonomy by decreasing dependence on individual family members. But more important, insurance decreases the tendency of any member of the insurance group to decide that someone else's life is not worth living. It is thus within the context of public and private insurance, as well as the current dominance of managed care, that many of the tough rationing decisions are likely to be made. The more important change that must take place is, ironically, in the general public—the patients or soon-to-be patients.

PUBLIC POLICYMAKING IN A GLOBAL CONTEXT

The Oregon Death With Dignity Act is premised on the ideology of autonomy and professionalism. There is an ironic aspect to this. The law purports not only to give people a "right" to death, something that will happen eventually to all of them, but also to confer "dignity" on the future event. It presupposes that those with terminal conditions who ask for a physician's prescription are more "dignified" in their dying than if they use Derek Humphry's suicide manual, *Final Exit*, to establish the lethal dosage of drugs. If the statute provides support for their "autonomy," it raises the question of what is "autonomous" about dying with the assistance of a physician's prescription pen? It should be clear that the question makes an investigation of the appropriate relationship of ideology to public policy. If people embrace both concepts of "individualism" and "professionalism," they find the concepts conflict at some point. Resolution is found through institutional analysis.

To contemplate whether Oregon's Death With Dignity Act should be a model for other states, one should acknowledge that acceptance of physician-assisted patient death as a legal construct has an international dimension. Over the past ten years, the Dutch courts and medical professionals have taken a number of steps to institutionalize the practice of physician-assisted death.

There are differences in the way medicine and law are organized in the United States and in the Netherlands. First, the Netherlands's medical system has been dominated for a long time by the idea of each patient having his or her own "primary-care" physician and nearly universal health care insurance. As a result, economic motives have not yet entered the realm of end-of-life decision making.[16] Although America is moving towards a system of "primary-care physicians," they are products of this country's own particular history and of America's social, legal, and economic organization of health care. Americans and the Dutch both believe that they, as individuals, are "autonomous" when they become patients, but those beliefs have different consequences because the medical contexts are different.

Second, in the Dutch legal system, physician-assisted death remains a crime on the books, yet is openly practiced under legislatively approved professional guidelines.[17] This apparent inconsistency is explained by the roles legislatures and other legal institutions perform in their system. In simple terms, courts and legislatures have a different institutional arrangement than Americans are accustomed to thinking about. In our system, judges dominate popular notions of what law is.

Yet, the institutional arrangements between judges and legislatures in the United States are matters that deeply divide people. The larger lesson is that all institutional processes—even political ones—have limitations in bringing about social solutions. It would be virtually impossible to import the Dutch system of law into our own on this issue, or any other. This international aspect of the public policy debate raises questions about whether this ideology should be translated into legislation in states other than Oregon in the United States. It also suggests the very real limitations we acknowledge in the process of creating public policy in a truly dynamic democratic society.

A commission established by the Michigan legislature to be "representative" and openly study the problem of assisted suicide declared it was "concerned over obtaining sufficient input from various communities (racial, cultural, disability) which were under represented on the Commission itself or might reflect personal life experiences markedly different from those of the Commission members."[18] While the commission tried to overcome this perceived deficiency in its own processes, in the end the commissioners acknowledged that the issue of assisted suicide might appear very different to members of racial and ethnic minorities or persons with disabilities than to organizationally embedded members of the commission. Unfortunately, the commissioners did not perceive that "interest group politics" always leaves open the question of indifference. While the highly interested will write and appear before the commission, the making of public policy often requires consideration of those who express indifference in the face of what special interest groups consider a matter of "life or death." The manner in which the issue is framed disenfranchises some, so decision makers must always be making public policy with a sense of the imperfections of any process they might choose.

CONCLUSION

Those physicians who seek to step beyond the constraints of law in actively aiding patient deaths should do so without public approbation. Where law has authorized physician aid in dying, as in Oregon, perhaps laity and physicians face a peculiar challenge. Will physicians encourage patient self-care, and will patients take those institutional steps such as purchasing long-term care insurance, when physician-administered death is an option?

My hope is, of course, that Oregonians will join the rest of the nation in recognizing the dangers in the road upon which they have embarked. Repeal of a voter initiative is not the solution, nor is declaring the voter initiative unconstitutional. Rather, the solution is constraint on the part of both physicians and patients in using that which the law has authorized. Oregon physicians will, for instance, join in the apparent move by the American Medical Association to improve the quality of pain care available. Oregon legislators, along with others, will have to consider if the present restrictions on some form of prescriptions need to be modified. One of the limitations in the Oregon Death With Dignity Act is that a person must be a resident of Oregon to be eligible for assisted suicide. Physician adherence to this legal restriction should prevent out-of-staters intent on self-determined timing of their death from flowing to Oregon to die, as Janet Adkins left Oregon to find Kevorkian in 1990.

Even before the United States Supreme Court issued its opinion on physician-assisted suicide, some members of Congress took a page from the abortion debate by suggesting that federal Medicare or Medicaid funds should not be used to cover the barbiturates used in physician-assisted suicide as authorized by the Oregon Death With Dignity Act. This proposal, finally enacted into law in 1997,[19] should remind us once again that cost containment, and thereby the rationing of health care, are still vigorous parts of the political and economic agenda in the United States.

Thus, the real focus of the legislative debate we now face after the Court's decision is not death, but dying and our fear of the process of dying. Most of us are ill-equipped to be present through the long process of another's dying on an hourly or even daily basis. Dying erodes our own sense of order of the social universe, leading to our need for institutional responses: hospitals, retirement "communities," nursing homes, hospice programs, and residential facilities.

NOTES

1. Virginia Woolf, *Three Guineas* (New York: Penguin, 1938), 20.

2. Martha C. Nussbaum, *Poetic Justice: The Literary Imagination and Public Life* (Boston: Beacon Press, 1995), 56–86.

3. See Einer Elhauge, "Allocating Health Care Morally," *California Law Review* 82 (1994): 449–544. Elhauge notes that other industrialized nations, such as Britain and Sweden, have introduced market reforms which are moving them toward cost containment. See ibid., n.1.

4. "Indicators: Health Care Spending," *OECD Observer* 215 (January 1999): 50.

5. *World Health Statistics Annual 1996* (Geneva: World Health Organization, 1998).

6. Physicians will need the assistance of other "experts" to create such systems in the more complex and dynamic economic environment. For instance, within so-called "capitated systems"—where physicians are paid a fixed amount for each patient for whom they serve as the primary-care provider—physicians should invite professionals with expertise in "total quality service" to become an integral part of their professional practices. These finance managers will help physicians serve their many "customers"—who include not just patients, but government reimbursement officials and managers from managed care companies.

Physicians as sole practitioners—as independent small business persons—or in partnerships with a few other similarly trained specialists may become economically unviable. Pediatricians, internists, and family practitioners—three distinct medical specialities—might consider forming partnerships, because managed care companies classify all as potential "primary-care physicians." These cross-specialty professional combinations may provide the organizational setting for achieving both monetary efficiency and effective patient care. See generally, Einer Elhauge, "Allocating Health Care Morally," 473–74.

7. See generally Paula A. Rochon, "Drug Therapy," *Lancet* 346 (July 1, 1995): 32–36 for the inadequacy of pain managment education and guidelines for physicians. Compounding the problem is the fact that health care providers are rarely accurate in their impressions of how much pain their patients are experiencing, particularly when that pain is severe. See, for example, Stuart A. Grossman et al., "Correlation of Patient and Caregiver Ratings of Cancer Pain," *Journal of Pain Symptom and Management* 6 (February 6, 1991): 53–57 (finding that nurses, house officers, and oncology fellows correctly assessed pain levels in their cancer patients 7 percent, 20 percent, and 27 percent of the time, respectively).

8. Other theories of breach of physician-patient fiduciary duty are developing in recent years. One patient, whose blood cells contained a rare form of DNA,

sued his physician for selling his blood to drug manufacturers for profit. The Supreme Court of California held that the physician had a duty to inform his patient of his financial interest in obtaining his blood samples, not just to obtain his informed consent in use of his tissue for diagnostic testing. See *Moore v. Regents of the University of California*, 51 Cal. 3d 120, 793 Pd 471, 271 Cal. Rptr. 146 (1990).

9. See generally Jay Katz, *The Silent World of Doctor and Patient* (New York: Free Press, 1986).

10. Or. Rev. Stat. § 127.280 (3.02).

11. See Malcolm Gladwell, "The New Age of Man," *The New Yorker* (September 30, 1996): 56–67.

12. Ibid., 58.

13. Ibid., 65.

14. Deliberate indifference of prison personnel to a prisoner's serious illness or injury constitutes "cruel and unusual punishment" under the Eighth Amendment. See *Estelle v. Gamble*, 429 U.S. 97 (1976).

15. Bernard Guyer, "Annual Summary of Vital Statistics—1995," *Pediatrics* 98 (December 1996): 1007–19, Table 8.

16. Paul J. van der Maas et al., "Euthanasia, Physician-Assisted Suicide, and Other Medical Practices Involving the End of Life in the Netherlands, 1990–1995," *New England Journal of Medicine* 335 (November 28, 1996): 1699–705.

17. Gerrit van der Wal et al., "Evaluation of Notification Procedure for Physician-Assisted Death in the Netherlands," *New England Journal of Medicine* 335 (November 28, 1996): 1706–11.

18. *Final Report of the Michigan Commission on Death & Dying* (Lansing, MI: The Commission, 1994), Part, History of the Commission [unnumbered].

19. *Assisted Suicide Funding Restriction Act of 1997*, Public Law No. 105–12.

Selected Bibliography

BOOKS

Andrews, Lori B. *The Clone Age: Adventures in the New World of Reproductive Technology*. New York: Henry Holt and Company, 1999.

Areen, Judith C.; King, Patricia A.; Goldberg, Steven; Capron, Alexander M. *Law, Science, and Medicine*. Mineola, NY: Foundation Press, 1984.

Burt, Robert A. *Taking Care of Strangers: The Role of Law in Doctor-Patient Relations*. New York: Free Press, 1979.

Carter, Stephen L. *The Dissent of the Governed: A Meditation on Law, Religion, and Loyalty*. Cambridge, MA: Harvard University Press, 1998.

Cohen, Cynthia B., ed. *New Ways of Making Babies: The Case of Egg Donation*. Bloomington, IN: Indiana University Press, 1996.

Dolgin, Janet L. *Defining the Family: Law, Technology, and Reproduction in an Uneasy Age*. New York: New York University Press, 1997.

Dworkin, Ronald. *Law's Empire*. Cambridge, MA: Belknap Press, 1986.

———. *Life's Dominion: An Argument about Abortion, Euthanasia, and Individual Freedom*. New York: Vintage Books, 1994.

Harris, Whitney R. *Tyranny on Trial: The Evidence at Nuremburg*. Dallas: Southern Methodist University Press, 1954.

Humphry, Derek. *Final Exit: The Practicalities of Self-Deliverance and Assisted Suicide for the Dying*. Eugene, OR: Hemlock Society, 1990.

———. *Lawful Exit: The Limits of Freedom for Help in Dying*. Johnson City, OR: The Norris Lane Press, 1993.

Humphry, Derek; Clement, Mary. *Freedom to Die: People, Politics, and the Right-to-Die Movement*. New York: St. Martin's Press, 1998.

Jones, James H. *Bad Blood: The Tuskegee Syphilis Experiment*. New York: Free Press, 1993.

Katz, Jay. *Experimentation with Human Beings: The Authority of the Investigator, Subject, Professions, and the State in the Human Experimentation Process*. New York: Russell Sage, 1972.

———. *The Silent World of Doctor and Patient*. New York: Free Press, 1986.

Kevorkian, Jack. *Prescription Medicide: The Goodness of Planned Death*. Buffalo, NY: Prometheus Books, 1991.

Komesar, Neil K. *Imperfect Alternatives: Choosing Institutions in Law, Economics and Public Policy*. Chicago: University Chicago Press, 1994.

Lifton, Robert. *The Nazi Doctors: Medical Killing and the Psychology of Genocide*. New York: Basic Books, 1986.

May, William F. *The Patient's Ordeal*. Bloomington, IN: Indiana University Press, 1991.

———. *The Physician's Covenant: Images of the Healer in Medical Ethics*. Philadelphia, PA: The Westminster Press, 1983.

Murdoch, Iris. *The Sovereignty of Good*. London: Routledge & K. Paul, 1970.

Naumann, Bernd; Steinberg, Jean, trans. *Auschwitz*. New York: Praeger, 1966.

Nuland, Sherwin B. *How We Die: Reflections on Life's Final Chapter*. New York: A. A. Knopf, 1994.

Nussbaum, Martha C. *Poetic Justice: The Literary Imagination and Public Life*. Boston: Beacon Press, 1995.

Palmer, Larry I. *Law, Medicine, and Social Justice*. Louisville, KY: Westminster/ John Knox Press, 1989.

Pollack, Robert. *Signs of Life: The Language and Meaning of DNA*. New York: Houghton Mifflin Company, 1994.

Posner, Gerald L.; Ware, John. *Mengele: The Complete Story*. New York: McGraw-Hill, 1986.

Price, Reynolds. *A Whole New Life*. New York: Atheneum, 1994.

Quill, Timothy E. *Death and Dignity: Making Choices and Taking Charge*. New York: W. W. Norton, 1993.

———. *A Midwife Through the Dying Process: Stories of Healing and Hard Choices at the End of Life*. Baltimore, MD: The Johns Hopkins University Press, 1996.

Rothman, David J. *Strangers at the Bedside: A History of How Law and Bioethics Transformed Medical Decisionmaking*. New York: Basic Books, 1991.

Scalia, Antonin. *A Matter of Interpretation: Federal Courts and the Law: An Essay*. Princeton, NJ: Princeton University Press, 1997.

Schlozman, Kay; Tierney, John. *Organized Interests and American Democracy*. New York: Harper & Row, 1986.

Schön, Donald. *The Reflective Practitioner: How Professionals Think in Action*. New York: Basic Books, 1983.

Wriston, Walter B. *The Twilight of Sovereignty: How the Information Revolution Is Transforming Our World*. New York: Scribner, 1992.

ARTICLES

American Medical Association Council on Ethical and Judicial Affairs. "Ethical Issues in Managed Care." *Journal of the American Medical Association* 273 (January 25, 1995): 330–35.

Andrews, Lori B. "The Sperminator." *New York Times Magazine*, March 28, 1999.

Bachman, J. G. "Attitudes of Michigan Physicians and the Public toward Legalizing Physician-Assisted Suicide and Voluntary Euthanasia." *New England Journal of Medicine* 334 (February 1, 1996): 303–9.

"Board of Directors Report on the Council on Legal and Public Affairs." *American Journal of Health System Pharmacists* 56 (1999): 652–59.

Burt, Robert A. "The Supreme Court Speaks: Not Assisted Suicide but a Constitutional Right to Palliative Care." *New England Journal of Medicine* 337 (October 23, 1997): 1234–36.

Chin, Arthur E.; Hedberg, Katrina; Higginson, Grant K.; Fleming, David W. "Legalized Physician-Assisted Suicide in Oregon—The First Year's Experience." *New England Journal of Medicine* 340 (February 18, 1999): 577–83.

Cockburn, Patrick. "CIA Destroyed Files on Radiation Victims; The Public May Never Know Full Details of Secret Experiments on Americans during the Cold War." *The Independent* (January 5, 1994): 10.

Cohen, Jonathan S.; Fihn, Stephan D.; Boyko, Edward J.; Jonsen, Albert R.; Wood, Robert W. "Attitudes toward Assisted Suicide and Euthanasia among Physicians in Washington State." *New England Journal of Medicine* 331 (July 14, 1994): 89–94.

Curriden, Mark. "Inmate's Last Wish Is to Donate Kidney." *American Bar Association Journal* 82 (June 1996): 26.

Dauer, Edward A.; Leff, Arthur Allen. "The Lawyer's Friend." *Yale Law Journal* 86 (1977): 573–84.

Dworkin, Ronald. "Assisted Suicide: The Philosophers' Brief." *The New York Review of Books* 44 (1997): 41–47.

Elhauge, Einer. "Allocating Health Care Morally." *California Law Review* 82 (December 1994): 1449–544.

———. "Does Interest Group Theory Justify More Intrusive Judicial Review?" *Yale Law Journal* 101 (1991): 66–87.

Elliott, K.; Foley, K. M. "Neurologic Pain Syndromes in Patients with Cancer." *Critical Care Clinician* 6 (April 1990): 393–420.

Epstein, Richard A. "Surrogacy: The Case for Full Contractual Enforcement." *Virginia Law Review* 81 (1995): 2305–41.

Eskridge, William; Frickey, Phillip. "Statutory Interpretation as Practical Reasoning." *Stanford Law Review* 42 (1990): 321–84.

Fried, Charles. "The Lawyer As Friend: The Moral Foundations of the Lawyer-Client Relationship." *Yale Law Journal* 85 (1976): 1060–89.

Gladwell, Malcolm. "The New Age of Man." *The New Yorker* (September 30, 1996): 56–67.

Grossman, Stuart A.; Sheidler, Vivian R.; Swedeen, Karen; Mucenski, John; Piantadosi, Steven. "Correlation of Patient and Caregiver Ratings of Cancer

Pain." *Journal of Pain and Symptom Management* 6 (February 6, 1991): 53–57.

"It's Over, Debbie." *Journal of the American Medical Association* 259 (January 8, 1988): 272.

Johnson, Sandra H. "Disciplinary Actions and Pain Relief: Analysis of the Pain Relief Act." *Journal of Law, Medicine, & Ethics* 24 (1996): 319–27.

Kahn, Patricia. "Genetic Diversity Project Tries Again." *Science* 266 (1994): 720–22.

Komesar, Neil K. "Taking Institutions Seriously: Introduction to a Strategy for Constitutional Analysis." *University of Chicago Law Review* 51 (1984): 366–446.

Lee, Melinda A.; Nelson, Heidi D.; Tilden, Virginia P.; Ganzini, Linda; Schmidt, Terri A.; Tolle, Susan W. "Legalizing Assisted Suicide—Views of Physicians in Oregon." *New England Journal of Medicine* 334 (February 1, 1996): 310–15.

Offit, Kenneth; Gilewski, Teresa; McGuire, Peter; Schluger, Alice; Hampel, Heather; Brown, Karen; Swensen, Jeff; Neuhausen, Susan; Skolnick, Mark; Norton, Larry; Goldgar, David. "Germline BRCA1 185delAG Mutations in Jewish Women with Breast Cancer." *Lancet* 347 (June 15, 1996): 1643–45.

Olansky, Sidney; Simpson, Lloyd; Schuman, Stanley. "Environmental Factors in the Tuskegee Study of Untreated Syphilis." *Public Health Reports* 69 (1954): 691–98.

Palmer, Larry I. "Life, Death, and Public Policy." Review of *Imperfect Alternatives: Choosing Institutions in Law, Economics, and Public Policy*, by Neil K. Komesar. *Cornell Law Review* 81 (1995): 161–80.

———. "Paying for Suffering: The Problem of Human Experimentation." *Maryland Law Review* 56 (1998): 604–23.

Quill, T. E.; Cassel, C. K.; Meier, D. E. "Care of the Hopelessly Ill: Potential Clinical Criteria for Physician-Assisted Suicide." *New England Journal of Medicine* 327 (November 5, 1992): 1380–84.

Quill, Timothy E. "The Care of Last Resort." *New York Times*, July 23, 1994.

———. "Death and Dignity: A Case of Individualized Decision Making," *New England Journal of Medicine* 324 (March 7, 1991): 691–94.

———. "Utilization of Nasogastric Feeding Tubes in a Group of Chronically Ill, Elderly Patients in a Community Hospital." *Archives of Internal Medicine* 149 (1989): 1937–41.

Rachlinski, Jeffrey J. "A Positive Psychological Theory of Judging in Hindsight." *University of Chicago Law Review* 65 (1998): 571–625.

Robertson, John A. "Liberty, Identity, and Human Cloning." *Texas Law Review* 76 (1998): 1371–456.

Rochon, Paula A. "Drug Therapy." *Lancet* 346 (July 1, 1995): 32–36.

Rockwell, Donald H.; Yobs, Anne Roof; Moore, M. Brittain. "The Tuskegee Study of Untreated Syphilis: The 30th Year of Observation." *Archives of Internal Medicine* 114 (1961): 792–98.

Rost, K.; Roter, D.; Quill, T. "Physician-Patient Familiarity and Patient Recall of Medication Changes." *Family Medicine* 22 (November-December 1990): 453–57.

Rupp, M. T.; Isenhower, H. L. "Pharmacists' Attitudes toward Physician-Assisted Suicide." *American Journal of Hospital Pharmacy* 51 (January 1, 1994): 69–74.

Schacter, Jane S. "The Pursuit of 'Popular Intent': Interpretive Dilemmas in Direct Democracy." *Yale Law Journal* 105 (1995): 107–76.

Shepherd, Lois. "Dignity and Autonomy After *Washington v. Glucksberg*: An Essay about Abortion, Death, and Crime." *Cornell Journal of Law and Public Policy* 7 (1998): 431–66.

————. "Sophie's Choices: Medical and Legal Responses to Suffering." *Notre Dame Law Review* 72 (1996): 103–56.

Shultz, Marjorie Maguire. "From Informed Consent to Patient Choice: A New Protected Interest." *Yale Law Journal* 95 (1985): 219–99.

The Study to Understand Prognoses and Preferences for Outcomes and Risks of Treatments (SUPPORT). "A Controlled Trial to Improve Care for Seriously Ill Hospitalized Patients." *Journal of the American Medical Association* 274 (November 22–29, 1995): 1591–98.

van der Maas, Paul J.; van der Wal, Gerrit; Haverkate, Ilinka; de Graaff, Carmen L. M.; Kester, John G. C.; Onwuteaka-Philipsen, Bregje; van der Heide, Agnes; Bosma, Jacqueline M.; Willems, Dick L. "Euthanasia, Physician-Assisted Suicide, and Other Medical Practices Involving the End of Life in the Netherlands, 1990–1995." *New England Journal of Medicine* 335 (November 28, 1996): 1699–1705.

van der Wal, Gerrit; van der Maas, Paul J.; Bosma, Jacqueline M.; Onwuteaka-Philipsen, Bregje D.; Willems, Dick L.; Haverkate, Ilinka; Kostense, Piet J. "Evaluation of the Notification Procedure for Physician-Assisted Death in the Netherlands." *New England Journal of Medicine* 335 (November 28, 1996): 1706–11.

Vonderlehr, R. A.; Clark, Taliaferro; Wenger, O. C.; Heller, J. H., Jr. "Untreated Syphilis in the Male Negro: A Comparative Study of Treated and Untreated Cases." *Venereal Disease Information* 17 (1936): 260–65.

Wellington, Harry H. "Common Law Rules and Constitutional Double Standards: Some Notes on Adjudication." *Yale Law Journal* 83 (1973): 221–311.

Wilkes, Paul. "The Next Pro-Lifers." *New York Times Magazine*, July 21, 1996.

Zaychikov, Evgeny. "Mapping of Catalytic Residues in the RNA Polymerase Active Center." *Science* 273 (July 5, 1996): 107–9.

REPORTS AND MISCELLANEOUS

Final Report of the Advisory Committee on Human Radiation Experiments. Washington, DC: Government Printing Office, 1995.

Final Report of the Michigan Commission on Death & Dying. Lansing, MI: The Commission, 1994.

Miss Evers' Boys. Home Box Office, 1997.

New York State Task Force on Life and the Law. *When Death Is Sought: Assisted Suicide and Euthanasia in the Medical Context*, May 1994.

Palmer, Larry I. *Study Guide for Discussion Leaders, Susceptible to Kindness: Miss*

Evers' Boys *and the Tuskegee Syphilis Study*. Ithaca, NY: Cornell University, 1994.

Welsome, Eileen. Testimony in U.S. Congress, House. *Hearings on Energy and Power Federal Government Testing of Human Subjects for Studies of the Effect of Radiation*. 103rd Cong., January 18, 1994.

Index

About the Author

LARRY I. PALMER is Professor of Law at Cornell Law School in Ithaca, New York, where he has taught courses on law and medicine for many years. He is the author of *Law, Medicine, and Social Justice* (1989) and numerous journal articles dealing with law, medicine, and policy. He is executive producer and author of the study guide for the award-winning educational video, *Susceptible to Kindness: Miss Evers' Boys and the Tuskegee Syphilis Study* (1994).